THE GOOD APPLE PUPPET BOOK

OVER 100 PROJECTS - puppets to make-stages-plays-songs-poems-games

by Juel Krisvoy

illustrated by Juel Krisvoy

Copyright © Good Apple, Inc., 1981

ISBN No. 0-86653-033-9

Printing No. 987654321

GOOD APPLE, INC.
BOX 299
CARTHAGE, IL 62321

All Rights Reserved - Printed in the United States of America by Hamilton Press, Inc., Hamilton, IL.

I

CONTENTS...

1

A NOTE TO TEACHERS:

When I was asked to teach crafts to two and three-year-old children, I realized they would need a great deal of individual instruction. The four-year-old children were easier to teach. Each day I began by setting up our room with a variety of free-play activity areas that I could keep an eye on while teaching crafts. Then three children at a time were asked to come to my work table (until every child had a turn). Two children watched while the third child finished one small piece of his weekly project. Then the remaining two children had their turns. Each day another small piece of the project was quickly finished. At the end of the week each child had something that he did most of the work on to take home and proudly show to his family. This daily discipline of early learning did not harm any of the children's creative abilities at all. In fact, the weekly projects were springboards to creating all kinds of new ideas on their own. Scissors were the most difficult to manage. Groups of ten children at a table practiced cutting up newspapers and creating their own unusual shapes. Have fun.

FIFTEEN PUPPETS FOR PRESCHOOL CHILDREN

THE THEATER

The stage for these preschool puppets is a simple-to-make cardboard picture frame.

Use a 16" x 20" piece of cardboard or poster board.

With a ruler create a 3" border on all edges of the sheet of cardboard.

Use a box cutter or a mat knife to cut out the center section.

Bend two wire coat hangers in half as shown in the illustration. Tape the hangers to the back of the frame. This will allow the picture frame stage to stand.

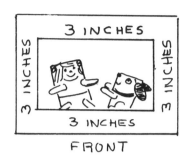

FRONT

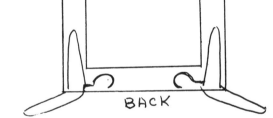

BACK

ENVELOPE PUPPETS

GIRL PUPPET

Seal an envelope.

Draw and color a girl similar to the one shown.

Cut four holes in the envelope as shown. Two fingers of one hand become the arms. Two fingers of the other hand become the legs.

3

DOG PUPPET

Seal an envelope.

Draw eyes, nose and mouth on the envelope and color each.

The eyes, nose and mouth, as well as back legs and a collar, should be drawn on both sides of the envelope.

Cut two ears and a tail from brown construction paper. Glue to the envelope with dabs of white glue.

Make one hole for one finger to stick through. The other finger stays on the other side of the envelope as shown.

ELEPHANT PUPPET

Seal an envelope, then draw and color the elephant.

Cut out two ears, a tail and a trunk from paper. Color them and attach them to the envelope with dabs of white glue.

Make two holes at the bottom of the envelope. The middle finger of each hand should be placed through each of the two holes. The middle fingers and the index fingers will create the legs of the elephant. Now the elephant will be able to walk, skip and hop about.

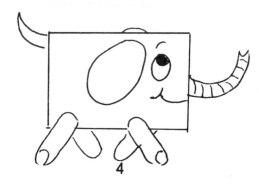

4

PAPER CUP PUPPETS

TWO PAPER CUPS ARE A DANCING PUPPET LADY

You will need two paper cups to begin this project.

Make one hole in the center of the bottom of each paper cup.

Place the two bottoms of the paper cups together.

Make a small loop at the end of a long chenille stem (pipe cleaner). Then push the straight end of the stem through the two holes.

The loop now holds the bottom cup in place.

Bend the stem a little at the closed bottom of the top cup. This holds the top cup securely against the bottom cup.

The remainder of the stem should protrude out the top of the open cup and should serve as a handle. The handle can always be bent a little for better gripping.

Hold the handle and make the puppet dance.

The puppet will be complete after a face, hair, arms, etc., are added. Markers can be used to add the facial features. Bits of colored construction paper could be cut and glued.

Yarn could be used for hair.

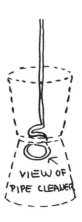

VIEW OF
PIPE CLEANER

TALKING CLOWN CUP PUPPET

Place the open tops of two paper cups against each other. Tape the two cups together on back side to serve as a hinge that can open and shut the mouth of the puppet on the opposite side.

Using a red marker, draw the lips along the tops of the two cups and draw a red nose. Using a black marker, draw two eyes and eyebrows.

OPEN AND CLOSE MOUTH.

BACK VIEW

Cut and glue on two paper ears. Then cut a two-inch strip of crepe paper that will extend around the entire paper cup. Glue below one edge to create the appearance of a ruffled collar around the clown's neck.

Then cut a three-inch strip of crepe paper that will extend around the bottom of the cup (the clown's head) and glue to cup. Press paper together near the top and tie with a ribbon to bring hat to a point.

Holding the hat with one hand and the bottom cup with the other, you can open and close the clown's mouth to make him talk.

6

PAPER CUP PUPPET

Again, you will need two paper cups for this puppet.

THE BODY: Place one cup upside down on a table and make a hole in the center of the bottom.

THE HEAD: Lay the second cup on its side and make a hole near the top. Then make another hole exactly on the opposite side of the cup.

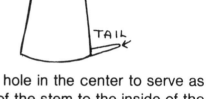

Poke a chenille stem through the hole in the center to serve as the tail of the pup. Tape the rest of the stem to the inside of the cup.

Attach the head cup to the body by guiding the stem through the two holes in the cup. Fold the remaining stem against the top outside of the head and form it into two ears to secure the head to the body.

Draw eyes, nose and mouth with marker. You can also draw a collar and legs. Holding the cup rim near the tail, you can make your puppet move.

DINOSAUR PUPPET

Make a cardboard pattern of a dinosaur. Instruct your children to trace the dinosaur twice on construction paper and cut out both patterns.

Put white glue on all of one dinosaur except on the legs. Place a pipe cleaner in the center of the body allowing half of the pipe cleaner to extend out the bottom to serve as a handle.

Then place the other dinosaur on top of the first and press the two together. Allow to dry completely.

DRAW ON HIS EYES AND HIS SMILE WITH A MARKER. Move the dinosaur about by holding on to his handle. He is ready to play.

PAPER CAT PUPPET

Fold a five-inch square of construction paper in half. Draw the legs and stomach lines (see picture). Cut out the shaded area, *double thickness*, through the paper. Tape or staple a pipe cleaner inside, with the remaining part below as a handle.

HEAD: Draw a circle with two ears. Cut it out and glue the head in place with white glue. See the picture. Draw the face and stripes with black marker. Cut out a striped tail and glue it on the back. She is ready to play.

PAPER BUNNY PUPPET

BODY: Fold a five-inch square of construction paper in half. Draw legs and stomach lines on each side.
HEAD: Draw two ovals exactly the same shape on the remaining construction paper with a bunny ear on each. Use a pattern you make for this. Draw the eyes, nose and mouth, etc. Glue together with the front top corner of the body staying inside of the head.
Glue cotton on the back for a tail.
Tape or staple a pipe cleaner inside the body with the remaining piece coming out of the body as a handle to move your bunny about.

A HOUND PUPPET

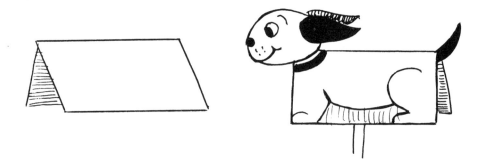

BODY: Fold a five-inch square of construction paper in half. Draw on the legs. Cut out the shaded area through the double thickness of the paper. Tape or staple a pipe cleaner inside the body, with the remaining part extending below as a handle to hold him.

HEAD: Draw two ovals (exactly the same shape) on the remaining construction paper. Cut them out and glue them together with the front top corner of the body inside of the head. Draw on the eyes, nose, mouth and collar.

Cut out darker paper ears and tail and glue them on. Now you can play with your hound puppet.

SANTA CLAUS PUPPET

The Santa head is a paper cup. Turn it upside down and draw hair and whiskers on the face, or glue on cotton whiskers and hair.

10

SANTA'S BODY: Use an empty toilet paper tube. Make a hole for *each arm.*
Fold a long chenille stem in half. Let the two ends come out of the two holes as arms.(The rest of the stem is inside of the tube.) Fold over the extra chenille stem ends to give thickness to the arms.
Paint the arms and body red and the boots and belt black. Let dry.
Put white glue *inside* the *back* of the cup head.
Place the *cup* on top of the *body.* Press the glued back of the cup head against the body and hold it until it is dry.

THE HAT: Cut out a 3-inch wide strip of red crepe paper long enough to encircle the head. Glue it on. Glue a cotton piece on the top of the hat to close it.
Glue on cotton collar and cuffs. Tape a pipe cleaner stem inside body and extend below as a handle to hold him.

A BIG FRIENDLY REINDEER PUPPET

The reindeer head is an empty toilet tissue tube. Draw eyes, nose, mouth, and ears on both sides with markers.

HORNS: Cut a slit on *top* of the *head between* the ears. Fold one chenille stem in half. Put the *folded end* into the slit and tape it in place *inside* the head. Bend the horns into wiggly shapes for a humorous effect.
NECK: Use an empty towel tube. Cut a slit on top of tube for the *head* to fit into. Tape it firmly inside. See illustration.   Your deer is finished. Hold on to him at the *bottom of tube.*

HALLOWEEN WITCH AND GHOST FRIEND

BODY OF WITCH: Use one toilet tissue tube. Cut out a piece of black construction paper to glue on to the tube body.
ARMS: Cut out one strip of the black paper to become 2 arms.

Glue each end onto the body so the center stands away from the body.

PUPPET HANDLE: Take one chenille stem and tape it inside the body with a piece extending below as the handle. The rest of the stem extends OUT OF THE TOP TO GO INSIDE OF THE HEAD.

THE HEAD: Cut out two matching circles of paper for the head. Color one side orange for hair in back. Draw witch face on other paper circle. Glue head pieces together with stem top inside.

HANDS: Cut out one small circle of flesh-colored paper. Glue it to the center of the arms.

WITCH'S BROOM: It is one pipe cleaner, taped behind the hands. Cut out small piece of yellow crepe paper to finish the broom. Fold one end of pipe cleaner broom handle over it to hold it in place.

WITCH'S HAT: Cut out two triangles, with brim shapes, from black construction paper. Glue them together with the top of the witch's head inside of the hat.

GHOST FRIEND: Draw ghost friend on white paper. Cut out and tape pipe cleaner on back to become a handle to hold him and play.

BUTTERFLY PUPPET

BODY: Cut out one plastic cup from an egg carton. Turn it upside down to become the *body* of the butterfly.

Fold one long chenille stem in half. Make two holes on *top* of the body where the *wings* should be attached. Push the two ends of the stem up through the *two holes* from *inside* the egg cup for the wings to fasten to.

HANDLE: Leave part of the folded end of the stem to extend out of the open cup below to hold the butterfly.

WINGS: Cut out 2 construction paper wings. Decorate both sides. *Staple chenille stems inside wings.*

HEAD: Make two tiny holes on top of head for thin wire feelers to come through. Fold a piece of thin wire in half. Push wire ends through holes. *Fold* of wire is taped inside cup. Bend wire tips. Draw butterfly face with thin marker. Butterfly is ready to play with you.

A TURTLE PUPPET

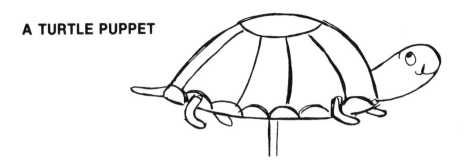

BODY: Cut out one egg cup from a plastic egg carton. Turn it upside down.

LEGS: Make 4 holes in the body for the legs. Push a pipe cleaner (colored green) through the front two holes to become the front 2 legs. Push another pipe cleaner (colored green) through the back 2 holes as the back legs. Fold over the 4 tips of the legs as feet.

HEAD AND TAIL:

Make a hole in front of cup for the head and a hole in back for the tail. Push another pipe cleaner through the two holes for head and tail.

HEAD: Cut out two matching head pieces. Glue the two head pieces on top of the front pipe cleaner. Paint the turtle green. Let dry. Paint on face.

HANDLE: Take another pipe cleaner and fold one end over to tape inside shell. The remaining part of pipe cleaner is bent down as the handle. Hold the handle and move the turtle about.

PAPER TUBE PUPPETS

A CAT: Take a piece of paper and form it into a tube...Staple the edges together (large enough to slip your hand

inside). Now draw the cat's head and four legs with crayons.

EARS: Color and cut out two ears. Glue in place.

TAIL: Color a paper tail and staple it in place.

RIBBON: Color a long strip of paper and glue it around her neck. She is finished. Your hand goes in through the bottom opening of the tube.

AN OWL: Form a piece into a tube. Staple the edges together to fit your hand.

Draw owl's head and body and color both sides.

WINGS: Draw and color them on a separate paper. Cut wings out and glue them to the body. Your hand slips in through the bottom and two of your fingers stick out of the top of the owl's head and wiggle as the owl's ears.

A MAN: Take a piece of paper and form it into a tube by stapling the two back edges together so the tube will fit over your hand. Draw and color the man's head and body on both sides with markers or crayons. On separate paper draw, color and cut out two ears. Glue them on. Cut out two holes in front for your fingers to come out as arms.

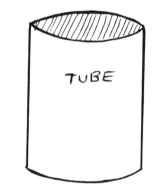

TUBE

A LADY: Construct the lady the same way you did the man. Draw and color her head and dress. Cut out two holes in front for your fingers to come out as arms. Now you can put your two hands inside of the two tube puppets and put on a puppet show. Try to create your *own* puppets this way. Make tube puppets of people that you know.

18

PAPER STICK PUPPETS WITH A THEATER

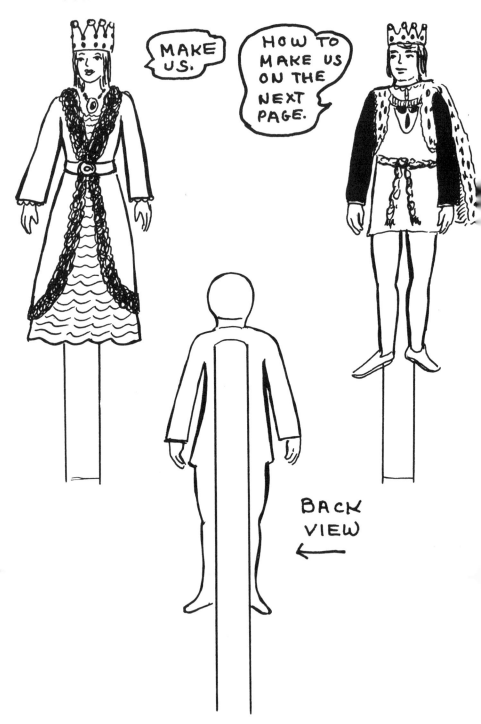

HOW TO MAKE THE STICK PUPPETS:

ANY STICK PUPPET: Make a stick puppet out of construction paper. Draw any person or animal on it. Color it and cut it out.
HANDLE: Make a cardboard handle and staple it on the back to hold the puppet from below.

HOW TO MAKE A PRINCE: Copy a picture of a prince from a fairy tale book. Color and cut him out. See illustration. Staple a cardboard strip on back of him as a handle to hold him from below.

HOW TO MAKE A PRINCESS: Copy her from a fairy tale book,too. Color her and cut her out, then staple a cardboard handle on back of her, too.

EXTRA CLOTHES TO MAKE: Trace around the shape of the prince with a pencil for his costume. Draw a loop at the top. Color the costume and cut it out. Cut out the loop center to slip over his head, and bend it back to hold on costume. The dress for the princess is a rectangle of cloth or crepe paper twice her dress length. Fold in half. Cut out a neck opening on dress, then fold to slip over her head. Tie a ribbon around her waist. See the illustration on the next page.

MAKE NEW CLOTHES FOR THE STICK PUPPETS.

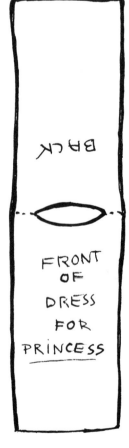

A DRAGON

Copy a DRAGON from a fairy tale book or copy this DRAGON. Color and cut him out. You may need to staple two sticks behind the legs to hold him.

A GIANT

He must be much taller and wider than the prince or princess. A giant always adds excitement to a story. Give him an angry and scary face. Draw him on construction paper and cut him out. Make sure that the cardboard stick is stapled high enough on the back to support him in his villain part acting with the prince and princess.

PIPE CLEANER

BACK

GIANT

A GIFT BOX THEATER (MADE FROM A GIFT BOX)

THE THEATER

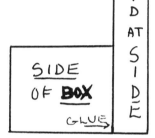

Remove the lid from a large gift box. Cut out most of the two sides that face you. Then cut out the center of the lid to make an open stage. Glue the open, standing lid to the front of the box (with the box fitting inside the lid). Decorate the lid in front to look like a theater. The puppets, worked from behind, now appear in the opening of the lid.

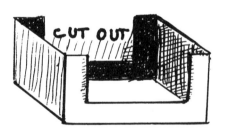

Note: The box sides are cut down to be out of the way of the puppets operating and not to obstruct the view in front. This is quick, simple and fun to do.

PAPER MIT PUPPETS

Note: When making these puppets always have the body large enough for your hand to slip into mit.

A MONSTER

Cut out two identical shapes of your own designed monster. Color the front and back, then glue his head and arm pieces together. Glue together only the two side edges of his costume and feet.

This leaves the center space empty so that your hand can slip into the puppet's body from below. A few staples might be added to reinforce him.

A GHOST

Cut out two simple ghost shapes. Glue the head, arms, and side edges together. This leaves room for your hand to slip in from below.

A LION

Draw and cut out two identically designed lion shapes. Color the front and back of the lion, then glue his head and arm pieces together. Glue only the two side edges of the body together. This leaves room in the center space for your hand to slip into the puppet below.

A HIPPO

Cut out two identical hippo shapes. Leave out the ruffle for now. Color the front and back. Glue head, arm pieces and body edges together. Your hand slips in from below (the unglued area).

RUFFLE: Glue a strip of crepe paper around the hippo's neck as a ruffle.

PAPIER-MÂCHÉ PUPPETS MADE OVER STYROFOAM BALLS

PEOPLE PUPPETS

Mix up a sticky paste of flour and water. Cut newspapers into small strips.
HEAD: Start it with a styrofoam ball. Cut a hole in the bottom for your finger to fit into the ball. This will hold the puppet while you work on it.
PUPPET WORKSTAND: Turn an empty facial tissue box upside down. Roll up a newspaper to a stick size. Make a hole in the box to hold the newspaper stick. Place the hole of the head onto the top of this stick. Dip a strip of newspaper into the sticky paste and apply it to the head. Continue dipping strip after strip into the paste and apply each strip to the head. Push in where the eyes will be. A small piece can be stuck on as a nose. Cut a slit for the mouth with a knife. Add papier-mâché ears. Let dry, then cut strips of white paper towel. Dip into the paste and cover head with one layer of these paper towel strips.

Add white tissue paper strips dipped in paste to build up cheeks if you wish. Let dry. Paint with flesh color acrylic paint. (Mix a little orange into white for flesh color.) Paint on the features. Use buttons, sequins or marbles for eyes. Glue on with airplane glue.

HAIR: Glue on strips of yarn with white glue.

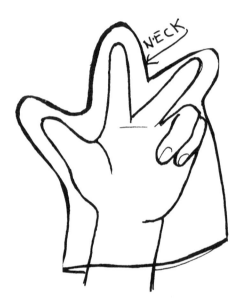

COSTUME: It should look like this shape. Cut out two that match from a material you like. Glue neck into neckhole or leave it unglued to change costumes. Sew edges together to second piece but leave the bottom open for your hand to go inside to move puppet.

MIT HANDS: Cut out two felt mit-shaped hands, two for each hand. Glue edges. Bottom is open. Paint flesh color and sew them to bottoms of each sleeve. Your fingers go inside to move them. Now you can animate your puppets with hand and arm motions.

A LION

Use the same basic styrofoam ball head but before covering it with papier-mâché, add a nose by cutting out a plastic carton egg cup. Hold the cup in place with hairpins pressed through the cup rim and into the head (styrofoam ball). Cut two dents in head to insert cardboard ears. Make indentions for the eyes. Don't forget the hole at the bottom for your finger. Cover him with papier-mâché method described. Paint him tan or yellow ochre mixed with white. Paint felt paws to match. Glue on a brown yarn mane. Sew a felt, painted tail onto the costume. Put yarn on tip of tail. (You could also use an orange mane.)

A PIG

Make a hole in the bottom of a styrofoam ball for your fingers. The SNOUT is a tube-shaped piece of cardboard, taped together and pressed into head with hair.

31

EARS: Cut two dents to hold two cardboard ears.
Hold with hair-pins pressed into head. Cover the pig with papier-mâché as described. Follow all steps. When dry, paint head and felt paws flesh color. Glue on eyes.

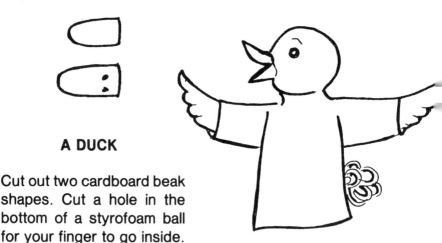

A DUCK

Cut out two cardboard beak shapes. Cut a hole in the bottom of a styrofoam ball for your finger to go inside.
Also cut two slits for beak. Put beak into slits, hold with hairpins in ball...make two dents for EYES. Cover with papier-mâché. Let dry, then paint white. Paint beak orange. Glue on two black button eyes. His costume is made like the others. Sew on white felt wings and a white yarn tail.

A DOG

NOSE: Cut out a plastic egg cup from an empty egg carton and fasten it to the styrofoam ball (head) with hairpins pressed around the edges into the ball. Don't forget to make a hole at the bottom for your finger. Make two dents for the eyes. Set the head on its stand. Papier-mâché is not put on to cover the entire head as previously described. Let dry, then paint the dog beige (burnt sienna mixed with white). Glue on two black button eyes with airplane glue. Paint on the nose and a happy smile.

EARS: Cut out two brown felt ears and glue on.

COSTUME: Use the original pattern described. Sew on beige-painted felt paws and brown felt tail. He is now ready to play.

NOTE: Details for all papier-mâché puppets made over styrofoam balls described in the beginning of this section.

FOIL: The same procedure is used as for papier-mâché used over styrofoam balls. The HOLE for your finger is shaped as you work with the foil. Foil does not need separate pieces for noses on animals, etc. Foil can be shaped into any type of head needed to cover with papier-mâché.

A TIGER

Form a foil ball with space left at the bottom for your finger to hold the head. Make a dent across the eyeline and dents for two eyes. Cover the head with papier-mâché procedure as described. Form ears and let dry on the stand. PAINT THE TIGER, sides and back of head and ears, orange. When it dries, paint white on front of face and black stripes and features. He has orange-painted felt paws described in the beginning.

EYES: Glue on green or yellow eyes. Paint black in centers.

TIGER SUIT: Use same pattern that you used for the other puppets. Sew on an orange felt tail with black stripes painted on it.

A WITCH

Form an elongated foil ball for her head. Make a hole for your finger on the bottom. Make two dents for her eyes. Place her on your stand. Proceed with papier-mâché covering. Form a hooked nose and pointed chin of papier-mâché to make her "witchier." After her head dries, paint her flesh color. Give her a rosy nose and cheeks. Paint on a mouth. Let dry.

EYES: Use old pearl earrings to make her scary. Paint eye centers green with a black spot in each. Glue on with airplane glue.

HAIR: Glue on orange yarn strips with white glue.

HANDS: Cut out pink felt mitten shapes, two for each hand. Glue around the side and top edge. Sew on to ends of sleeves on costume.

COSTUME: Use the same costume pattern originally described. Make it black. Add a black cape if you like.

MAKE A DOLL PUPPET (See picture of doll with the witch shown above.)

DOLL HEAD: Form a round ball of foil. Make a hole at the bottom for your finger to go in. Dent in a bit where the eyes will be. Proceed with papier-mâché method and when nearly finished, use some tissue paper strips dipped into paste to form doll's round cheeks.

Form a small chin and nose the same way and paste them on doll face. Let dry. Paint the face flesh color and nose, chin and cheeks rosy. Also paint on a smile.

EYES: Make them large, blue sequins or buttons glued on with airplane glue.

HAIR: Glue on strands of yarn with white glue.

DRESS: Use pattern previously described.

HANDS: Sew on pink felt mitten hands glued around the edges (side and top) as described.

A FROG

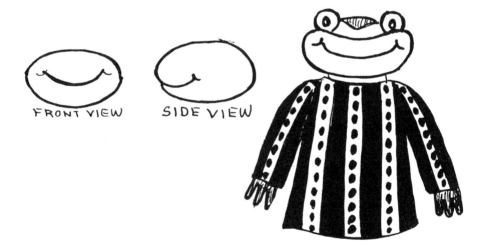

FRONT VIEW   SIDE VIEW

FROG HEAD: Form an oval of foil. Make a hole at the bottom for your finger. Then cover his head with papier-mâché. Also form two places at the top to hold the frog's eyes.
MOUTH: Roll up two strips of paper dipped in paste. These strips form the mouth. Paste it in place.

When dry, paint mouth yellow and
the rest of the frog green.

EYES: Use two large white buttons with centers painted black.
Glue buttons in place with airplane
glue.

GREEN FELT HANDS are sewed onto the bottom of his
costume. Make costume from same basic pattern as the
other papier-mâché puppets described in beginning.

Create your own puppet ideas to act out stories children like
to read. Now they can be acted out on your own puppet
stage.

CREPE PAPER PUPPETS

RAG DOLL

HEAD: Cut rectangle of pink crepe paper the length of your two hands.

NECK: Make a small cardboard tube for neck. Tape together. Place facial tissues on top as a head stuffing. Fold pink rectangle of crepe paper in half over stuffing. Use cellophane tape to seal pink crepe paper at bottom of tube. Fold excess paper in back of head and glue. This leaves front of face smooth.

FACIAL FEATURES: Draw eyes, nose and mouth on separate paper. Cut them out and glue onto face. Use white glue. Make it a cute face with personality.

HAIR: Crepe paper pieces with a fringe cut on the bottom and glued onto the head.

DRESS: Cut out two of these crepe paper shapes as her dress. Glue together along the arrows. Let glue dry.

PUT ON DRESS: Slip the doll's neck into the neck hole and glue it to the tube. Your hand goes in through the bottom of the skirt. One finger goes into the head. The thumb and third finger come out through the arms to become the hands. See hand position in illustration here.

This rag doll puppet is the basic way to make all crepe paper people puppets. You can make endless variations.

41

EASTER BUNNY

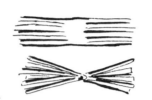

He is made of white crepe paper. Follow the same directions you basically did in making the doll.

THE WHISKERS: Use white paper. Cut fringes on each end, then twist in the center and glue them in place.

EARS: Each ear is two white pieces of crepe paper glued together over a pipe cleaner. Glue pink paper centers in the ears. Staple ears to head.
TIE: Glue on a paper bow tie and a cotton tail.

A FRIENDLY FISH

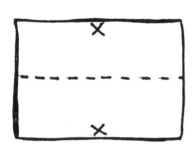

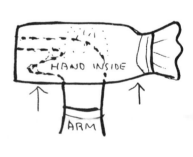

Cut a rectangle wide enough to cover your hand when folded over. Glue together at the arrows and tape around tail with cellophane tape. Your hand goes inside the fish, between the arrows. See picture above.

On white paper, draw two eyes, two fins and a spiny top piece. Color, cut out and glue on as illustrated. Your hand enters the fish through the bottom between the arrows and comes out the front to let your fingertips become the moving mouth.

A PUPPET OF "MEN"

You are on your own making this PUPPET, because it is made like the RAG DOLL PUPPET. If it is a boy just draw a line in the center where the skirt would be, then it will appear as a pair of pants. Have fun with this. If you can make the RAG DOLL PUPPET, you can easily make the "ME" PUPPET.

43

PAPER BAG HEAD PUPPETS

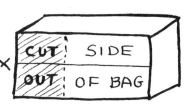

PONY PUPPET

Cut out section X on the side of a paper bag (lunch size). Place open X side over the closed end of a second bag. Glue in place with white glue.

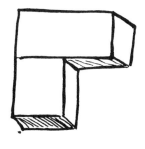

Glue on two paper ears. Draw on his face with markers. Cut out a fringed crepe paper mane. Glue it in place. Your hand goes inside from the open bottom. He is ready to play.

A WIGGLE NOSE

Use one paper bag (lunch size) for the head. Cut a slit for the nose to slide through. Cut out two identical noses from another paper bag. Glue the side edges together except the X ends. Slip the X ends of nose into slit on the bag. Tape X ends inside of bag.

FACE: Draw or paint the EYES and MOUTH on the BAG. Glue on the paper EARS and crepe paper hair.

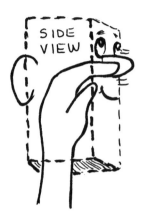

The picture shows how to use one finger inside the nose to make it move back and forth and wiggle.

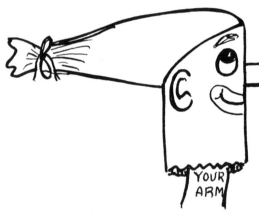

CLOWN PUPPET WITH A NOSE THAT GROWS

THE HEAD: Made from a paper bag. Cut a hole in front for the nose and another hole directly opposite it in the back. These holes are for the nose to pass through from the front to the back to make it appear longer and shorter.

46

CLOWN NOSE: The nose is a cardboard tube from a gift wrapping roll. Cut the length you need to make a long nose. Round off one end with scissors and staple it shut. Paint the nose red.

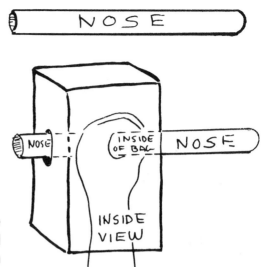

THE FACE: Paint on the eyes, eyebrows and a red mouth. Cut out and glue on paper ears. Push the nose through the two holes. Put your hand through the bottom of the bag. Circle your fingers loosely around the tube. The tube nose can now be pushed back and forth with your other hand outside of the head.

THE HAT: Take a rectangle of colorful cloth and sew the sides together. Glue or staple hat on back of the head. The hat will hide the back of the nose. Tie a ribbon on the end to bring it to a point to finish the hat.

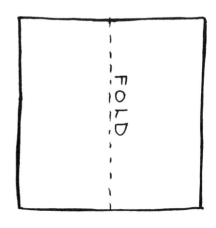

Now you push and pull
nose from the
outside of
the hat in
back.

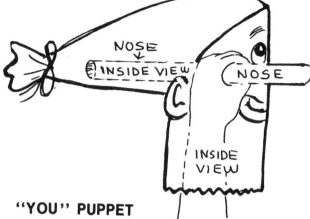

"YOU" PUPPET

Make a paper bag puppet head to look
like a friend. Cut out a double thickness
bag nose. Glue on face. Paint on eyes
and mouth. THE HAIR is crepe paper cut
with a fringe on the ends.

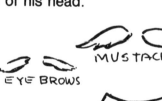

SANTA CLAUS PUPPET

HEAD: One paper bag becomes
Santa's head. The closed end of
bag is the top of his head.

BEARD: Cut out white
paper beard, mustache and
eyebrows. Glue them on
the face. Paint on eyes,
nose and his mouth.

48

SANTA'S HAIR: Cut out a rectangle of white paper long enough to cover sides and back of head. Cut a fringe along the bottom edge to look like hair. Glue the hair around the sides and back of Santa's head.

SANTA'S HAT: Cut a long enough red crepe paper rectangle to encircle Santa's head. Glue the hat around the top of Santa's head and also glue the remaining two back pieces together as a seam in back. Staple the top of the hat to make it pointed. Glue cotton around the bottom and a ball on top. Slip your hand into Santa's head from the open bottom of the bag. Have a Merry Christmas with your Santa Claus. Next, you can make Santa a reindeer.

SANTA'S REINDEER

Make the REINDEER as you basically made the PONY, from two paper bags (lunch size). His antlers are cut out of construction paper, double thickness if needed, and glued together with a pipe cleaner or a cardboard strip inside. Cut slits for the antlers on top of the head and tape them inside.

YOUR ARM

FACE: Paint on the eyes, nose and mouth. Your hand slips into the puppet through the open neck at the bottom.

EARS are cut out and pasted on.

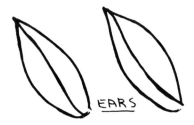

EARS

50

PAPER BAG BODY PUPPETS

HOUND DOG PUPPET

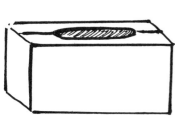 

BODY: Use one lunch size bag to make the body. Cut a hole in the bottom for your hand to slip inside.

HEAD: On a second bag draw two identical dog heads with necks. Cut them out and draw on the features. Glue them together but leave the ends of the neck unglued. Fold up the bottom of the neck pieces and glue them to the body where the head belongs.

EARS: Color, cut out and glue on two ears.

LEGS: Cut out two front legs and two back legs from a paper bag. Glue the legs onto the body.

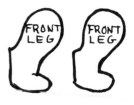

TAIL: Cut out and glue on.

BOW: Tie a crepe paper ribbon around the dog's neck.

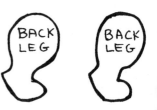

52

ELEPHANT

Use one paper bag for the head and body.

EYES: Draw them on white paper, cut out and glue on. Draw a big smile with a black marker.

THE TRUNK is two identical pieces glued together, almost to the bottom X marks, where the trunk begins. Glue X parts to the head in front.

EARS: Cut out two ears and glue onto the head.

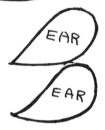

LEGS AND TAIL:

Draw and cut out four legs and a tail from part of a paper bag. Glue them on. Your hand goes in through the open bag at the bottom. Enjoy playing with him.

ZEBRA PUPPET

BODY: Use one lunch size paper bag. The closed end is the zebra's chest. Color the stripes black.

53

Cut a hole in the bottom of the body for your hand to go inside through the stomach.

HEAD: Draw and cut out two identical zebra heads with necks

and tabs. Glue the heads and necks together except at the tabs. Glue the tabs at the bottom of neck onto the body. Draw eyes, nose and mouth and black stripes.

LEGS: Draw two back legs and two front legs and draw on their stripes. Cut them out and glue them in place. TAIL: Cut out black crepe paper tail. Glue it on.

MANE: Cut a strip of black crepe paper. Cut fringe on edge and glue it on the neck. Your zebra is finished and ready to play with the other animal puppets.

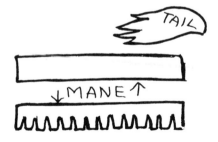

AIRPLANE PUPPET

A paper bag
becomes
the body
of the
plane.
Cut a hole on the
bottom for your

hand to go inside to hold the plane. Note that the creased side of the bag has become the bottom of the plane now.

FRONT WINGS AND TAIL: They are made from a second bag. Cut out two identical front wing pieces and glue them together. Then cut out two identical back tail pieces and glue them together. Fold the tail piece in half. About one inch down from the fold, staple it, and then turn up the two sides and glue onto the top end of the plane, to look like the picture above. Print name on front wings and glue on top of the plane. Put your hand inside and run and fly away.

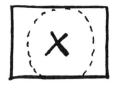

PEOPLE PAPER BAG PUPPETS

On the closed bottom of a paper lunch bag, make a circle the size of a puppet. Turn the bag over, so the X head is now on the top. Cut out only on the dotted line, then pull the X circle head up. (It is still attached to the bag in front.) Then staple the bag together by the X head, from front to back.

FACT: Draw a head on pink construction paper. Make the features and neck large enough to cover the X area on paper bag. Glue the face and neck on the X area. Glue on crepe paper hair.

THE ARMS: Cut two holes in front of the bag for two of your fingers to come out, as two arms of your puppet. Your hand goes through the open bottom of the bag.

CLOTHES: Color the bag as the dress or suit it wears. Make boy and girl puppets.

56

PAPER PLATE PUPPETS

SNOWMAN

Take two small paper plates and staple them to-gether around the rims. The backs of the plates face out. Draw the features with markers.

BODY: Staple two large paper plates around the rims, with the BACKS facing out. Draw buttons on the front. Cut out an oval shape in the back for your hand to go inside. Staple head to the body.

ARMS: Cut out two arms from heavy white paper. The end pieces marked X will become tabs in back to move the arms up and down. Make a hole in each arm near the X. Also make a hole for each arm on the snowman's body. See picture. Slip a paper fastener through the front hole of each arm to hold it on. Bend up the X tabs in back to grasp and move the arms.

SCARF: Decorate a long strip of paper to look like a scarf. Glue it around the snowman's neck.

HAT: Make two identical hat shapes. Color the outsides, then cut them out and glue them together over the head.

THE GNOME

Make him basically
as you did the
snowman, but color
his face and hands flesh
color and add ears.
Color his suit green and draw
on a brown leather belt.

HAT: Cut out two tall triangle shapes, color them red. Glue the hat shapes together over the top of his head.

BEARD: See picture above. Cut out a white paper beard and mustache and glue them on. Make other gnomes and write a little play about gnomes and perform for your friends. You can create your own gnome world such as in a storybook.

ANGEL

Make her basically as you did the SNOWMAN. Color her face and hands flesh color.

HER DRESS: Cut out two identical dress shapes and sleeves with hands to match. Color them.

WINGS: Cut out two yellow wings.

HALO: Color a pipe cleaner yellow; form one end into a circle halo and tape the stem on the back.

ANGEL'S HAIR: Cut out strips of yellow crepe paper and cut fringes on the the bottoms. Glue hair onto head. Your ANGEL IS FINISHED. Now she can greet your relatives and friends who come for a HOLIDAY visit.

HAIR

BANGS

DUCK

HEAD: Staple two small paper plates together around the rims. Have both plate backs facing out.

BODY: Fold one large paper plate in half. Staple together along the curved bottom. Leave an open space for your hand to slip into the body. Staple the head to the body at one end.

WINGS AND TAIL:

Cut out three squares of yellow crepe paper. Cut fringes on the end of each. Glue them on as two wings and a tail.

BEAK: Cut out two identical orange construction paper beaks. Glue together as a mouth for the duck.

LEGS: Cut out two orange construction paper legs. Glue them on either side of the opening for your hand.

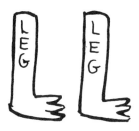

TURTLE

THE SHELL: Color the bottom of one paper plate yellow and the bottom of another paper plate green. Decorate the green plate to look like the top of a turtle shell. Staple the two plates together around the rims with the colored backs showing. Cut out an oval shape from the yellow plate for your hand to slip into. Cut a slit in front of the shell for the turtle's neck to fit into.

HEAD: Cut out two identically shaped turtle heads. Glue them together except the parts marked X. Slip the head into the slit. Spread the X parts of the neck apart and staple the neck to the bottom of the shell by the slit.

LEGS AND TAIL:
Cut out four green colored legs and tail....Staple them at the bottom of the shell so that the four legs and tail stick out. Slip your hand into the cutout oval at the bottom and you can play with your turtle puppet.

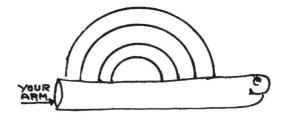

SNAIL

Take one small paper plate. On the back of the plate make a swirl design with crayons or paint.

Put white glue down one side of an old sock and press the glued part right across the center of the swirl on the plate. Keep your hand inside, so that the glue doesn't stick to the opposite side of the sock.

When the glue is dry, fold the plate in half. with the rims meeting and staple the rims together at the top.

Glue on felt eyes and cut two holes on top for fingers to come out as feelers.

The snail is ready to be a puppet and act for you in a performance.

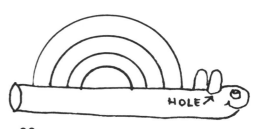

63

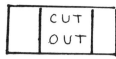

CEREAL BOX PUPPETS

ROBOT

Cut out all of the bottom of a cereal box, except a small space on each side.

HEAD: Two small paper plates with their backs facing out are stapled together around the rims, except a space left to cut out a neck shape. Draw on the face.

STICK HANDLE: Cut a strip the length of the box. Staple one end of the cardboard strip inside the neck opening of paper plate head.

ARMS: Cut a second strip of cardboard 6 inches wider than the width of the box. Cut a slit on each side of the box for arms to go in one slit and out the other.

Make a slit on top of the box. Push the stick handle through it. The attached head remains on top of box. Reach inside box and staple the stick to the arm bar inside at X mark (see picture). PAPER SHOES are glued on the bottom. Paint robot with white gesso. Let dry, then decorate and paint him.

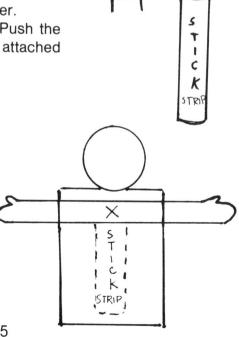

ASTRONAUT

Make the ASTRO-
NAUT with the same
procedure as the
ROBOT, but use larger
paper plates because
the HEAD is drawn and
colored inside the
plate's center. The
outside edge of the
plate becomes the
space helmet. The BODY is painted on the cereal box to
look like a space suit.

A BALLOON MAN

Make him
as you did
the ROBOT,
but with a
different head
and suit.
Long pipe
cleaners with
colored paper
balloons stapled
on top and the bottom
of the pipe cleaners
stapled to his hand
complete the BALLOON MAN.
Operate him as you do the
ROBOT, by holding onto the
stick handle inside of the body.

66

SHEEP

BODY: Turn an empty cereal box on its side; cut out indicated areas on both sides.

Opposite sides match. Cut out the bottom of box. This forms the legs. Then cut a 2-inch slit at the top of front and back of narrow body.

Cut a 2-inch wide cardboard strip long enough to go through the 2 slits and protrude out front and back. Cut the back end to form a TAIL.

HEAD: Draw head and neck on cardboard. Paint the face area black except the white eye parts and pink mouth. Staple head and neck to protruding front piece.

FEET: Paint them black.

SHEEP WOOL: Fold white crepe paper strips in half and cut slits along the fold to look like wool. Glue them all over the body and head except the black face and feet.

Hold the puppet by the strip inside the body.

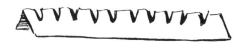

OLD-FASHIONED TUBE FINGER PUPPETS

PEOPLE PUPPETS

On heavy white paper draw, color and cut out a BOY and a GIRL with extra side pieces that you roll in. Fasten as a finger tube in back with tape. Your two fingers fit into the tubes to walk the puppets just like grandmother did as a child.

This is not a new idea but added to this book for those who have never seen them. You can make any kind of puppet character in this charming tiny size to fascinate children to act in a tiny homemade puppet theater. The rest of the puppets are original new ways for tiny ones.

PIPE CLEANER RING FINGER PUPPETS

Draw a COWBOY
on white heavy
paper. Color
and cut
him out.
Also draw a
TAP DANCER.
Don't draw her
legs because
your two

fingers are her legs. Color and cut her out.
FINGER RINGS: Fold a long chenille stem,
(about 11½ inches long) in half. Make a circle
at each end for your two fingers.....then staple
and tape them to the back of each puppet
(one for each).

MAKE THEM MOVE: Your two fingers go
into the two finger circles in the back to
make the COWBOY run and to make the
TAP DANCER dance. Her feet are your
fingers dancing on a table. Create some
new ring finger puppets as a pair of
dancers or funny clowns, any type you
like.

FINGER, PIPE CLEANER & TWO-SIDE PUPPETS

EASY PIPE CLEANER HANDLE PUPPETS

FAIRY TALE PUPPETS

These puppets are the easiest to make and to handle. Try to draw FAIRY TALE PEOPLE 4 inches tall. Color and cut them out. Fold a pipe cleaner into an L shape. Staple or tape it on the back as a HANDLE (one handle on back of each puppet). You can easily act out your favorite fairy tales with these simply made puppets. They will work well in the TOP HAT THEATER and CEREAL BOX THEATER described in this book.

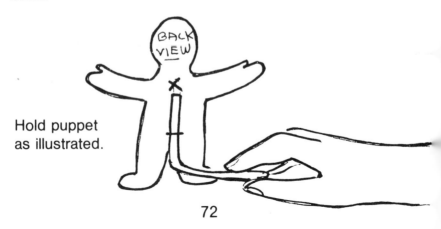

Hold puppet as illustrated.

72

TWO-SIDE PUPPETS
(AS FINGER PUPPETS)

Take two identically shaped
paper puppet pieces drawn
and colored on construc-
tion paper. Cut them out
and glue them together
around the top and side
edges. Let dry.

Then your finger can go in
from the bottom into the
unglued area to hold and
operate the puppet.

Choose NURSERY RHYME CHARACTERS and make them
this way. Act out a nursery rhyme and be creative. (Give
each a NEW ending that you make up.) Also say to the audience when you come near the end of a rhyme, "and then,
what happened?" The audience now comes up with new
creative endings to your chosen NURSERY RHYME. This is
fun for everyone and can be done with any rhyme.

A TOP HAT THEATER & CEREAL BOX THEATER

A TOP HAT THEATER

This little theater is good for finger puppets to dance, sing, recite poems and tell funny jokes, riddles, etc. Now let's make it.

Take one empty round oatmeal box and glue it to the center of a paper plate. Cut out an opening in the front to view the performing puppets. Then cut out another opening in the back to put the puppets through to perform. They are operated from the back. Before using the TOP HAT STAGE, paint it black. When the paint dries, glue a colorful ribbon (hat band) around the bottom of the hat by the brim.

CEREAL BOX THEATER

Use one large empty cereal box to make this theater. You can give tiny plays with tiny puppets in this theater. Use any of the described tiny fingers puppets to perform in this theater.

LET'S MAKE THE CEREAL BOX THEATER

Cut out an opening in front of the box to view the puppets. Also cut out the shaded area indicated in the picture, on the back of the box. This is for you to work the puppets seen in front. Cut two holes, one on each side, at the top near the back, for a dowel stick to hold a sheer black curtain backdrop, so the audience doesn't see you operating the puppets.

Paint the box with white gesso to block out the colors of the original cereal box. Let dry. Then paint the theater colorfully to look like a puppet theater. Colored papers can also be used. Glue them on for a similar effect on your theater.

BACKDROP: Reach in and glue the top of the sheer black curtain to the top of the dowel stick. Your cereal box theater is ready for a performance.

ROD PUPPETS

RODS: MAKE THEM FROM WIRE HANGERS, SPOKES, FLOWER STEMS, KNITTING NEEDLES, CHENILLE STEMS, WIRES, etc.

TIGER

Draw a tiger on heavy white cardboard. Color and cut him out.

RODS: On the back, tape two wire rods as shown in the picture. Alternating the back and front, move the tiger up and down, while holding one rod in each hand. This will make him walk and run.

MAGICIAN (WHO CHANGES FACES)

Cut out a cardboard HEAD, NECK, SHOULDERS and HANDLE as one piece. Paint hat black.

THE CAPE: Cut out two of these cape shapes and sew together on the dotted lines.

MAGICIAN'S CAPE SUIT

Sew the top of a ROD to the edge of the sleeve, then put on the MAGICIAN'S CAPE.

THE FACES: Cut out five white faces the identical shapes of magician's HEAD. Draw a different expression on each face. Staple them to the top of MAGICIAN HEAD like a pad of paper.

HOW TO PERFORM WITH THE MAGICIAN

Hold the handle with your right hand and the rod with your left hand. The MAGICIAN complains about his ugly face to the audience. Then he cries out the magic word, "FACE-BE-GONE!" He quickly turns his back to the audience, while the puppeteer reaches up with left hand still holding the rod and tears off the FIRST FACE and drops it behind the stage. The MAGICIAN turns around and faces the audience, then drops his arm to reveal a new FACE. "How do you like this?" he asks. A child is given a mirror that he holds up to the MAGI-CIAN. He complains all over again, "HORRIBLE! FACE-BE-GONE!" He covers face, turns around, repeats by tearing off the horrible face, and as before, reveals another face to discuss with the audience.

This is repeated until all five faces have been used. He finally turns around to reveal his original face, sighing and looking in the mirror again, "It's really not such a bad face after all, once you get used to it."

WITCH DOCTOR (WITH A GAME TO PLAY)

Cut out a cardboard HEAD, NECK, SHOULDERS, and HANDLE ·all in one piece. Then cut out a NOSE of paper, double thickness.

Glue the nose pieces together but spread out the beginning of the nose pieces to glue them on face.
PAINT ON A SCARY FACE and glue on crepe paper strips for hair. Paint and cut out HANDS to staple on costume.

COSTUME: Cut out two identical pieces of cloth, like the picture. Sew on the dotted line. Staple hands inside of the sleeves.

Sew ROD, at the top, to the end of the left sleeve (behind hand). Put costume on puppet.

THE WITCH DOCTOR GAME

Hold the puppet handle (inside costume) with your right hand. Hold the end of the ROD with left hand. The WITCH DOCTOR'S left hand waves back and forth over a large pot (prop) filled with imaginary brew. He says, "I see letters W, R, E, B....What do they mean?" The children try to guess what the mixed up letters spell. The answer is *BREW*. The child who guesses it can pick the next word to whisper to the WITCH DOCTOR to mix up and the children try to guess the new word. Continue playing the game as long as you like. You might even have the WITCH DOCTOR spell words backwards for variety. This can be educational and keep the children interested and alert to words, spelling and changes.

THE CREEPY THING

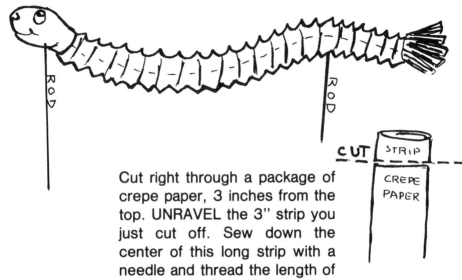

CUT STRIP

CREPE PAPER

Cut right through a package of crepe paper, 3 inches from the top. UNRAVEL the 3" strip you just cut off. Sew down the center of this long strip with a needle and thread the length of your CREEPY THING. Tie a knot at the end after you pull up the crepe paper into a ruffle to fit the length of your body piece of thread.

HEAD: Draw, color and cut out a funny head from a filing card. Staple head to one end of ruffle.

TAIL: Cut out a fringe from crepe paper to staple on the back end of body.

ATTACH RODS: Tape one rod to the back of the neck. Second rod, bend over the top about two inches. Weave the bent top into the crepe paper ruffle near the end. The rest of the rod comes down for you to hold it. The other hand holds the other rod. Move CREEPY THING UP AND DOWN TO MUSIC.

THE CREPE PAPER STRIP

SHADOW PUPPETS AND THEIR THEATERS

MR. BIRD AND BELINDA BIRD (SHADOW PUPPETS)

These SHADOW PUPPETS use transparent colors set into cardboard frames that you cut out.

BODY: Cut out a cardboard frame for the body and wings. In the center you have cut out, glue colorful crepe paper to fill the empty spaces. The colors are glued to the back of the frame.

HEAD AND BODY: Cut the head out of construction paper. Cut a hole for the eye. The NECK is a strip of colorful crepe paper. Belinda Bird has a crepe paper toppiece added. Glue it on.

TAIL: FEATHERS are strips of colored crepe paper stapled on. Cut out crepe paper legs and feet as pictured. Glue them onto body.

RODS: Bend the ends of two wire rods. Tape to the frame at a right angle to the body and back of head.

HOW TO PERFORM WITH THE BIRDS

The PUPPETS are held close to the back of an acetate-type (cloudy white) screen. Puppets are held by their two rods. A light must shine BEHIND and right THROUGH the puppet's transparent colors as you make the puppets dance, moving the rods to the music played from a tape or record. The audience sits in FRONT of the acetate screen to view the puppets illuminated from behind as colorful SHADOW PUPPETS dancing to the music.

NOTE: You also can use colored acetates, colored tissue papers or colored cellophane pieces or sheer colorful cloth in place of the crepe paper transparencies used in the BIRD frames. Sometimes opaque papers are cut out as shadow puppets. These opaque puppets appear behind the screen as silhouettes to the audience in front of screen. Some ancient shadow puppets were made that way.

EXPERIMENT, create all kinds of fantasy figures and creatures in frames. Try the opaque silhouettes, too.

SHADOW PUPPET

THEATERS

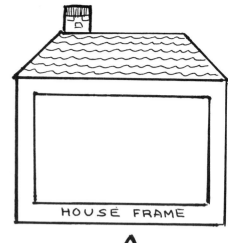

HOUSE FRAME

Your PUPPET THEATER SCREEN for SHADOW PUPPETS can be made of heavy cardboard. You can use a piece of cardboard 20 inches by 24 inches. Make this piece into a frame. Rule out 2½ inch borders on all four sides. Then with a mat knife cut out the center, leaving a frame. Cover the opening by gluing or taping acetate or thin white silk-like material inside the frame. This frame is then attached to an open doorway and is surrounded by curtains above, below and on the sides of the frame so that the light from the hall behind the frame shines brightly through the whitish acetate only.

CASTLE FRAME

CIRCUS FRAME

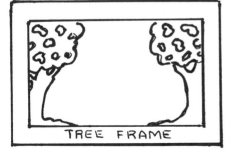

TREE FRAME

Attach the scene to the back of the acetate screen, so now the light from the hall shines right through, and the puppets can act in front of the illuminated background.

TRY REAR PROJECTION as another idea on the acetate screen or use a rear projection screen; project slides of scenes onto the back of the screen, focusing from behind it, while the puppets act in front of the screen with their footlights illuminating them. A moving picture could also be projected onto the back of the screen and seen in front as background. Also children could draw and color scenes on pieces of paper and by using an opaque projector, project the scene on back of the acetate screen. Puppets in all projects use footlights. Take it from here and you will come up with more creative ideas.

TWO SHADOW PUPPET POEMS TO ACT OUT SECTION

TWO SHADOW PUPPET POEMS TO ACT OUT

FISH, FISH, FISH.

(A narrator recites this poem while puppeteers move the fish and scenery behind the acetate screen of the puppet theater.)

FISH, FISH, FISH

1-A fish who was bigger made fun of the size
2-Of a fish who was smaller, and then a surprise!
3-A fish still much BIGGER, with a gleam in his eyes
4-Made the middle-sized fish feel so small and unwise.

Make 3 sizes of FISH, described on the next page. The 3 fish act out the matching acting numbers to the same numbered line of the poem. The scene opens with the smallest fish swimming happily about. NARRATOR speaks poem line (1) as the middle-sized fish swims in to tease the little fish. He pokes and pesters him. Line (2) The poor little fish escapes in terror. The middle-sized fish swims victoriously! Line (3) The biggest fish sees what happened to the little fish and swims in and frightens away the bully middle-sized fish. Line (4) The smallest fish gratefully returns to swim and play with the biggest fish who loves him.....(THE END)   (SEE THE NEXT PAGE)

HOW TO MAKE THE THREE FISH IN POEM

Cut out 3 cardboard
fish-shaped frames, small, medium
and large. Glue a different transparent colored paper in each
frame to fill each empty space. Their tails are strips of colorful crepe paper. Decorate with fine black marker. Tape a
ROD to the back of each fish to move him about.
Cut out scenic water plants as frames and glue transparent
green papers inside empty frame space. TAPE RODS to the
back of the frames to make them sway in the water.

A GIANT BLUE BUTTERFLY

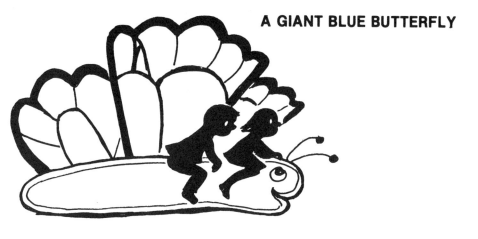

(1) There once lived two children who flew through the sky,
(2) On the back of a giant blue BUTTERFLY.
(3) They flew over trees of frosty, green lace,
(4) And lovely green hills all over the place.
(5) Look at the people, downb there on the earth.
(6) They're running around for all they are worth.
(7) Too busy, too busy, to stop and look out
(8) At the wonderful things that we see all about.

Make the BUTTERFLY with FRAME WINGS and body with transparent colorful centers. The CHILDREN sitting on the BUTTERFLY are made of construction paper silhouettes. A NARRATOR recites the POEM. A puppeteer operates the BUTTERFLY RODS with two hands and a second puppeteer moves the SCENERY as described. All is acted from behind an acetate screen.

HOW TO MOVE THE SCENERY AS THE POEM IS PER-FORMED

LINES (1 & 2): The BUTTERFLY, with CHILDREN, flies up and down, then hovers in one stationary spot.

LINE (3): TREE props move slowly up and down from the right side toward the left, as the audience views it. Then the trees move down and disappear. This gives the illusion that it is really the BUTTERFLY who is moving.

LINE (4): Then the GREEN HILLS prop appears in the same way, moving up from below stage on the right and traveling left, then down disappearing.

LINES (5, 6, & 7): Two sets of PEOPLE props appear from below and walk by crossing in front of each other, then disappear below.

LINE (8): The BUTTERFLY is now alone with the CHILDREN. A RAINBOW, PINK CLOUDS with happy faces and a smiling YELLOW SUN all are props with rods that appear and disappear near the BUTTERFLY who SIGHS, to end the poem.

HOW TO MAKE THE PUPPETS AND PROPS

THE GIANT BLUE BUTTERFLY: Cut out one body and wing frame, all in one piece. Leave space for the children to sit. Glue transparent BLUE paper in the open spaces, then draw eyes and decorations with fine black marker on the wings. Staple two fine wire feelers on top of the head.
MAKE A SECOND WING the same way. Tape the wing to the body like a hinge and tape a rod to the top of the wing. The other rod is taped to the BODY.
CHILDREN: CUT OUT OPAQUE SILHOUETTES, then staple them on top in front of hinged BUTTERFLY wing.

This second WING with its hinge enables you to move this wing back and forth with one hand holding its ROD. The other hand holds the body rod, which you use to tilt the body back and forth to make both wings appear to be moving when seen through the acetate screen.

SCENERY PROPS

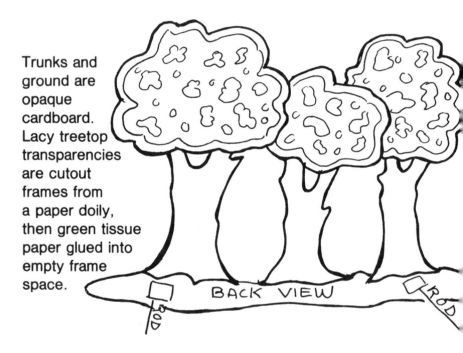

Trunks and ground are opaque cardboard. Lacy treetop transparencies are cutout frames from a paper doily, then green tissue paper glued into empty frame space.

BACK VIEW

HILLS: Cutout frames with green tissue paper glued inside. RODS are taped on each.

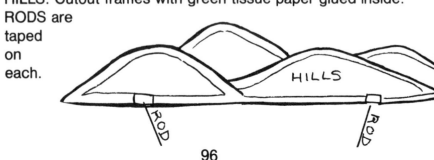

HILLS

RAINBOW for BLUE BUTTERFLY
Cut out transparent paper
arches and, with cellophane
tape, attach them to a
white tissue paper
arch that has
its cardboard
frame. Tape
two rods
on back
to move
rainbow.

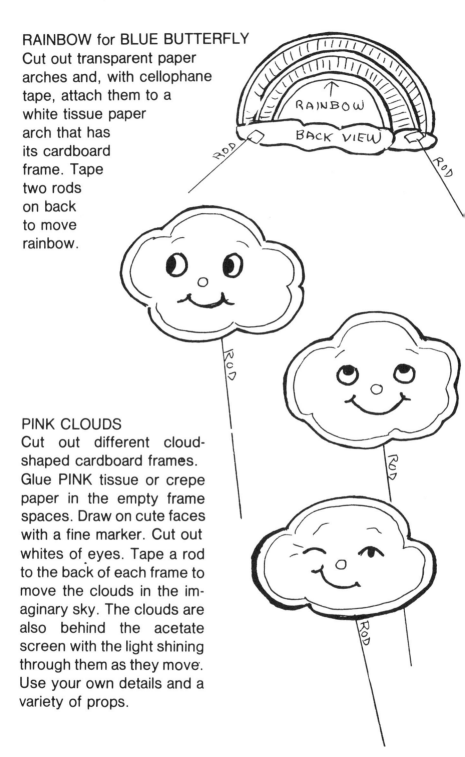

RAINBOW

BACK VIEW

ROD

ROD

ROD

ROD

ROD

PINK CLOUDS
Cut out different cloud-
shaped cardboard frames.
Glue PINK tissue or crepe
paper in the empty frame
spaces. Draw on cute faces
with a fine marker. Cut out
whites of eyes. Tape a rod
to the back of each frame to
move the clouds in the imaginary sky. The clouds are
also behind the acetate
screen with the light shining
through them as they move.
Use your own details and a
variety of props.

THE SMILING SUN PROP for THE GIANT BLUE BUTTERFLY

Cut out a round frame and glue yellow crepe paper in the open center space. Then glue an orange strip of crepe paper cut like a fringe around the outside of sun frame, as the sun's rays. Tape a ROD on back.

TWO SETS OF PEOPLE PROPS
Draw SILHOUETTES of a group of PEOPLE walking, attached to a strip of cardboard. Use black construction paper for the people. Make two people props - tape rods on back.

Note: Different shaped rod.

98

NOVELTY PUPPETS

MR. SNAPNOSE

Staple two large paper plates
together around the rims with the
plate BACKS facing out. Leave an unstapled space at the
bottom to put in the top of a cardboard TUBE. Glue it in with
white glue. Cut a hole in each plate for the NOSE to go
through. The NOSE is a "BLOWOUT" party favor. Push the
BLOWOUT mouthpiece through the front hole and directly
out the back plate hole.
Draw a face on the plate and glue on paper EARS and crepe
paper HAIR. Now he needs a HAT.
HAT: Cut out two identical paper hats and glue them
together, leaving the top of the head inside.
JACKET: Cut out two identical paper JACKETS and
decorate and glue together, leaving part of tube inside. Blow
out nose, behind head, as a surprise.

MR. HORNBIRD

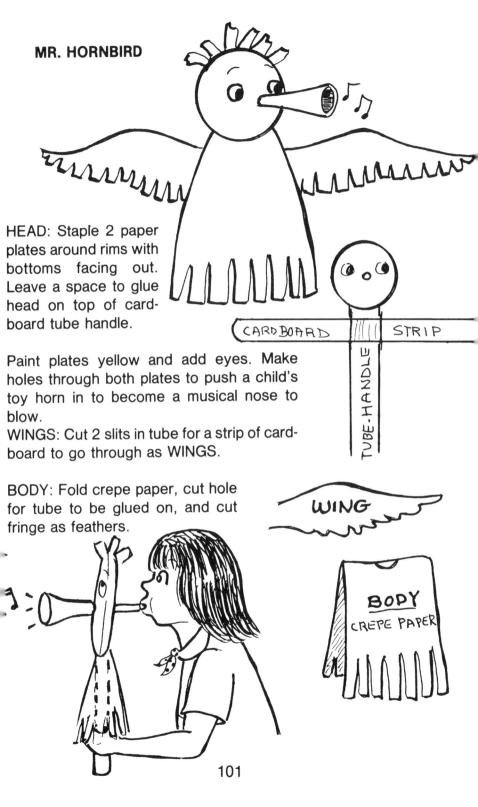

HEAD: Staple 2 paper plates around rims with bottoms facing out. Leave a space to glue head on top of cardboard tube handle.

Paint plates yellow and add eyes. Make holes through both plates to push a child's toy horn in to become a musical nose to blow.

WINGS: Cut 2 slits in tube for a strip of cardboard to go through as WINGS.

BODY: Fold crepe paper, cut hole for tube to be glued on, and cut fringe as feathers.

CARDBOARD STRIP

TUBE-HANDLE

WING

BODY CREPE PAPER

"I AM MR. TALL & MR. SHORT"

HEAD: Draw two identical heads with necks and shoulders.
Color faces and add eyes, nose, etc. Hair is crepe paper. Fold a chenille stem in half. Glue head pieces over fold of chenille stem, leaving the folded part inside head, except a small piece to hold puppet on top. See picture.

The two ends of chenille stem are twisted around the top of a SLINKY, sold in toy stores. (Use a small slinky.)
MAKE PUPPET TALL BY PULLING UP THE SLINKY.
....Make him SHORT by lowering the SLINKY.
PAPER FEET are attached at the bottom by folding heels over bottom. Staple.
BODY:
Identical shapes glued over the shoulder piece.
Children love these.

STAPLE

FOOT

102

MR. EGGHEAD

THE HEAD is
two plastic
egg cups cut from
an empty plastic egg
carton. Place the two open ends
of the two cups together. Put two pieces of cellophane tape,
one on each side of the head. This holds the cup rims
together like a hinge. See picture. Glue on pieces of crepe
paper for hair. The EYES, NOSE AND MOUTH, etc., are
drawn with fine black markers.

HIS JACKET: Cut a rectangle of
crepe paper or colorful cloth. Fold it
in half and cut a hole on the fold for
your finger to go through. Cut
another hole in the bottom of the
head.

Crook your finger inside and against the head to move his
mouth. Your other two fingers are the arms. Put on jacket so
his arms come out and one finger goes up into head as described. You can easily change his clothes for a new look.

CLOTH, FELT & POLYFOAM PUPPETS SECTION

CLOTH AND FELT AND POLYFOAM PUPPETS

"SWEETIE" THE ELEPHANT

Draw a paper PATTERN of the side view of the HEAD and BODY of an ELEPHANT. See illustration. Lay this PATTERN on a piece of cloth that is quilted cotton with a small design.

Trace this pattern twice on cloth. Cut out the two pieces and sew together, on wrong side of material, except in open spaces -1, 2, 3. Open spaces 1 and 2 are for the trunk to pass through. Open space 3 is for an oval piece of cloth cut out and sewed around where elephant sits. Dots show where to sew. Turn cloth inside out.

PAPER PATTERN

OPEN (FOR TRUNK) PEN
① ②

HEAD AND BODY SHAPE

(SIDE VIEW)

③ OPEN

TRUNK: Cut a rectangle of cloth as long as your arm and wide enough to wrap around your arm with seam allowance.

Sew the two long sides together to form a tube-shaped trunk.

HEAD

YOUR ARM INSIDE THE TRUNK

Sew trunk to head where they meet.
Then with scissors round off the end of the trunk.
Cut out oval piece of felt, fold in half and sew inside the rounded end of the trunk where your fingers go.
MOUTH: Cut out a smile from red felt.
Glue it onto the elephant right under the trunk.
STUFF HEAD above and below the trunk tube with polyester fiber (used in pillows). Put the stuffing inside through back of head where trunk goes in, then sew back opening to trunk after head and body are completely STUFFED with the polyester fiber.

EARS: Cut out two cloth and two felt matching pieces. Sew each cloth ear to its matching felt piece, then sew onto the head.
EYES: Cut out two oval white felt eyes, sew one black button in each eye, then glue felt eye to head.

LEGS: Cut out 4 cloth rectangles. Sew one edge of each to form 4 tubes. Cut 4 cloth oval shapes to sew onto bottom of each tube to become bottoms of feet.

Fill each leg with polyester fiber. Then sew the legs onto the elephant as illustrated.

TAIL: Cut out a rectangle and fold in half, then sew sides together to form a point. Sew onto elephant.

RUFFLE: If you should want a ruffle, cut out a long strip of felt, sew on one long edge, then pull thread to make a ruffle which you sew around the neck.

PEOPLE PUPPETS - TWO WAYS TO MAKE FELT HEADS:

Cut out 2 circles or 2 profiles and their necks of pink felt. Sew around edges, except at the bottom. Turn inside out and stuff with polyester fiber. Glue or sew on felt.

Glue on felt nose, felt smile and, if you wish, pink felt ears and yarn hair. Use buttons or sequins for eyes.

NOSE

NECK TUBE: Cut out a rectangle of cardboard the length of your finger and wide enough to wrap around your finger. Tape it into a tube shape. Then glue it inside the NECK.

BODY: Sew two pink rectangles together on the dotted line. Turn inside out and sew the NECK inside the neck opening of the body.

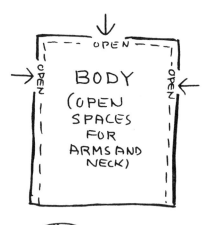

BODY
(OPEN SPACES FOR ARMS AND NECK)

OPEN

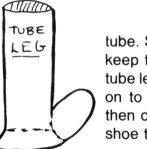

TUBE LEG

LEGS: Cut out 2 rectangles and sew each into a tube shape. Make the legs of felt. Turn the end of the leg up to become the foot on each tube. Sew through the bottom of each heel to keep the feet turned up. Stuff legs. Sew the tube legs to front bottom of the body. Glue felt on to make shoes. First glue on shoe tops, then cut out and glue on felt soles to join the shoe tops from below.

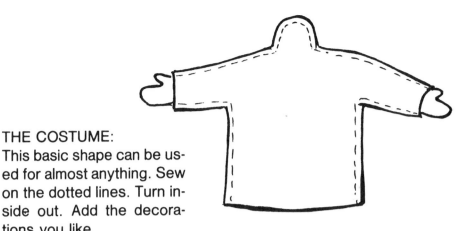

THE COSTUME:
This basic shape can be used for almost anything. Sew on the dotted lines. Turn inside out. Add the decorations you like.

HANDS: Cut out 4 identical mitten shapes from pink felt. Glue two together around the edges, except at the wrist. Space is left for your finger. Make another mitten hand the same way, then sew one to the bottom of each sleeve, allowing room for your finger to fit inside of each hand.

PANTS: Cut out two identical PANTS from cloth. Sew together on dotted line.

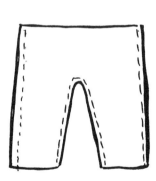

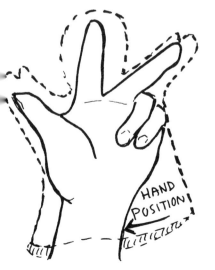

HAND POSITION

Turn inside out and sew to bottom of costume. You can make endless people this way with all kinds of heads.

HOLD PEOPLE THIS WAY.

109

A CALICO DOG (with a wagging tail)

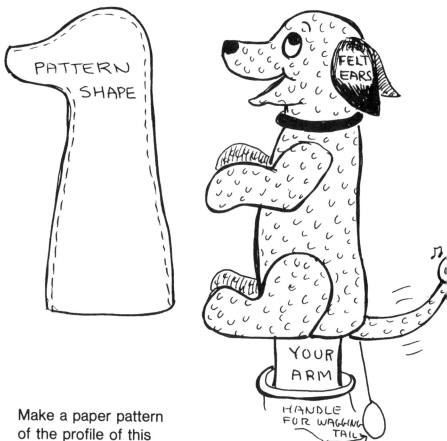

Make a paper pattern
of the profile of this
dog's head and body, about
15 inches long. Lay the pattern
on the reverse side of calico, quilted cotton material, trace it
then turn over the pattern and trace it again. Cut out two
pieces and sew together on the dotted lines. Turn inside out
so the calico now shows.

MOUTH: Cut out two bottom mouth parts, one red felt and
the other of calico. Sew along the dotted line, then turn inside out. The red felt is the bottom inside of mouth.

Cut another piece of red felt. This part is sewed

to the bottom red felt piece. Join the two straight edges and it will be the top inside part of mouth.

NOTE: When you sewed the dog's head and body seams, the bottom of the nose area was NOT to be sewed together.

This open space was left for the felt mouth you just completed. Now sew the red felt mouth inside the mouth. Cut out and glue on red felt tongue. Finish sewing and it will look like this.

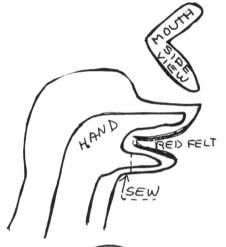

TOP OF HEAD: Cut one styrofoam ball in half and glue inside, to the top of the head. Also, have a piece of felt glued to the flat part of ball before it goes into the head.

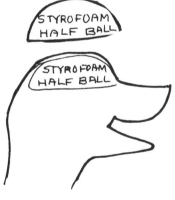

Sew on felt EARS. EYES and NOSE are felt glued on dog.

111

LEGS: You need four top leg pieces and four bottom leg pieces. Each leg has two identical pieces sewed together on the edges, on the reverse side. Turn the legs inside out so the calico will show. Then stuff each leg with polyester fiber. When finished, sew the legs onto the body. THE TAIL: Cut out two identical tail shapes. Use a piece of sculpture wire, with ends turned over and a little longer than the tail, to push inside tail, from the back, after the tail is sewed together. Turn the extra part of the tail wire downward, as a handle. Now you can sew the tail to the dog, and the handle wags the tail. Sew on a Christmas bell to its tail tip. Add a felt collar.

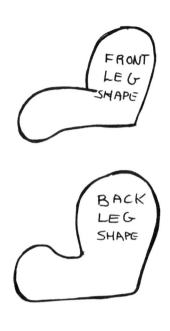

A CALICO CAT

See the directions for the PEOPLE PUPPETS. Use calico type quilted cotton material. Make the HEAD as directed, cut out four identically shaped EARS. Glue two together for each ear. Sew to head.

Cut out black felt EYES. Glue on or sew on shiny button eyes.

NOSE: Sew on a button. Whiskers are cut from an old whisk broom. Wind matching thread around the center and sew under the cat's NOSE. Glue on black felt mouth.

BODY: It is made like the people puppet body.

MOUTH

LEGS: They are made like the calico dog's legs. Tail is made like dog tail without the wire inside.

BOW: Sew on a felt ribbon and bow.

DUCK PUPPETS

Use fake yellow fur or a yellow hand towel to make a DUCK. Make a PATTERN of the profile view of a DUCK with the head and body all in one piece. Trace the pattern on the reverse side of the material. Turn over the pattern and trace it again. Sew it along the dotted line.

Turn the
puppets
inside
out so
the fur
shows.
Cut a
slit on
each side
for the
wings to
slip inside.
Use this duck pattern.

HEAD
AND
BODY
SHAPE
SIDE
VIEW

OPEN

WINGS: Cut out two matching oval shapes for each wing. Sew them together on the reverse side. Turn them inside out so that the fur side shows. Fold each wing in half, slip into the slit on either side of the body and sew in place. Put sculpture wire in wings to move them from the outside. See picture.

BEAK: Make a pattern for the larger upper beak and the smaller lower BEAK.

WING

FOLDED
WING

MOVE
WING
WIRE
WING

BEAK
TOP

BEAK
BOTTOM

114

UPPER BEAK: Cut out a large orange and a large black felt beak.

LOWER BEAK: Cut out a small orange and a small black felt beak. Stitch or glue the two parts of the upper beak around dotted line (orange felt on top). Do the same for the two small beaks (orange felt on bottom). See diagram. Slip pieces on fingers as shown in the picture. SEW BLACK FELT STRAIGHT EDGES TOGETHER (not the orange parts), forming inside of mouth. Sew orange parts of beak into the head opening. HALF OF A STYROFOAM BALL is glued inside head. See directions in doing this as done for dog.

TAIL: Sew on loops of yellow yarn.

EYES: Sew on black shiny buttons.

LEGS: See PEOPLE LEGS directions but make these orange. FEET are cut like this:

BOY DUCK'S HAT is made of two triangles glued together and sewed on head. A tassel is also sewed on. GIRL DUCK'S HAT: She wears a scarf triangle.

POLYFOAM PUPPETS

They are very popular and can be made in huge sizes and as rod puppets, too. They can be cut out of large blocks of polyfoam with various size scissors or carved like a sculptor carves. Also half-inch polyfoam pieces may be used for the easiest type of head.

SIMPLE HEAD: Trace two equal-sized circles and cut out of polyfoam. Then cut a pie-shaped wedge out of each. Glue the open edges of the open wedge together with rubber cement or contact cement.

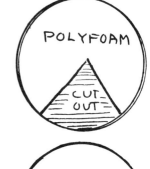

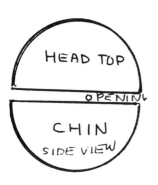

The part that was cut out becomes rounded. Press together when glue becomes sticky. Hold to dry.

MOUTH: Cut out a PATTERN of a circle shape that will fit inside the mouth after you fold it in half. Then trace this pattern onto a piece of cardboard and glue onto a piece of red felt.
Cut out both pieces and glue them together with white glue. Put polyfoam pieces together like picture. Glue X edges together on each side to act like a jaw hinge.

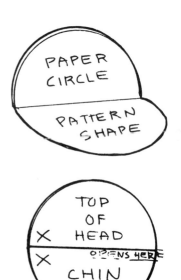

116

Open in back for hand - open front for mouth.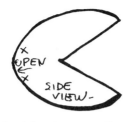

Your hand goes in the back between the two X marks. Leave enough room. Now fold the cardboard, red felt piece in half to become the inside of the mouth. Place it inside the mouth and glue or staple it around the edges of inserted mouth to the polyfoam edges of the mouth. Paint with acrylic paint.

THE COSTUME: Cut out two pieces; sew on dotted lines. Second costume needs tube arms and foam mitten hands. LEGS and arms are tubes made from a rectangle. Glue (or just cut out of polyfoam). SHOES can be two felt oval shapes sewed on edges, stuffed and sewed to the bottom of the tube legs or polyfoam painted ovals. Paint with acrylic or thinned out oil paint or spray paint. Then paint on features. (The nose can be cut out of polyfoam and glued on.) HAIR is yarn glued on to your liking.

EARS: If you should need ears that show, cut out polyfoam ears and paint them and glue on.

PUT THE POLYFOAM PUPPET
TOGETHER.

The front of the neck opening is sewed or stapled to the chin area in the back where your hand goes inside. The back of the neck area is sewed or stapled to the back of the top head piece of polyfoam above the opening where your hand goes into the head. The costume now has the head opening inside, so you enter the open bottom of the dress or jacket and reach your hand in through the head opening inside the costume.

SEW ON THE REMAINING PARTS, arms and legs, then sew rods to hands. (Old umbrella spokes may be used as rods.) NOTE: Use RUBBER CEMENT, since not all contact cements are dependable.

SOCK PUPPETS

DANCING FEET SOCK PUPPETS

HOW TO MAKE THEM: Use a pair of plain colored socks. Cut the EYES, NOSE, MOUTH, etc., out of FELT. Glue them on with white glue to make funny faces. Glue or sew on felt or yarn hair as you wish. EARS can be sewed or glued on, too.

HOW TO PERFORM WITH SOCK PUPPETS: Put the sock puppets on your feet. Lie down on your back with your feet facing the audience, so they are seen, dancing to a record as a curtain is held above.

GIRAFFE SOCK PUPPET

Use one long yellow sock. Cut out a red felt oval to fold in half. Put white glue on one side and push it into the toe of sock as a mouth. Hold it in place to dry. Sew on two BLACK BUTTON EYES and yellow felt EARS. Then cut a black felt strip as a MANE. Sew it down the back of neck. Cut slits along the edge like a fringe.

HORNS: Cut two little holes on top of head. Push a pipe cleaner in one hole and out the other; bend over each end and sew into head.

TAIL: Sew on yellow felt tail with black tip.

LEGS: Cut out four of yellow felt and sew them on. They just hang down from body.

ALL OVER GIRAFFE and black on each hoof. He is finished and ready to play. Put your arm inside the opening in back and your hand in the mouth to make it move. See the picture of girl and giraffe above.

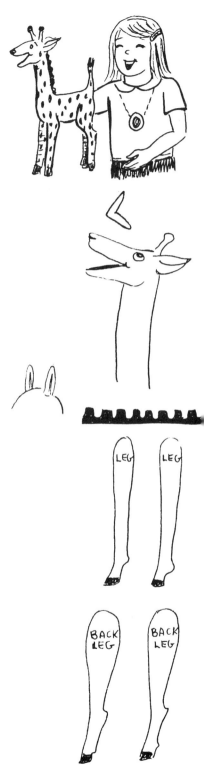

121

FLOWER SOCK PUPPET

THE HEAD: Sew two identical circles together around the edges, except for about 4 inches left as an opening. Turn head inside out. Stuff the head with polyester fiber. Put your hand and arm inside of a long green sock, then push the toe up into the head. Sew the sock where it meets the opening of the head to the head, to secure it. Cut out white felt circles for eyes and sew a black shiny button on each eye and then glue the eyes onto the face with white glue. Glue on a red felt smile and sew on a small gold button nose. Cut out and glue red felt flower petals protruding out from the face. They are glued on from the back. Two petals glued together for each petal are best. STEM WITH LEAVES: Cut two small holes in stem and push a pipe cleaner (colored green) through the holes. Cut out two felt leaves for each side. Glue two leaves together over the stem, leaving it inside. To move the puppet, slip your hand through the bottom opening of stem into the head.

ANTEATER SOCK PUPPET

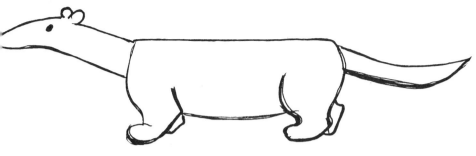

HOW TO MAKE IT: Use one long brown sock for the head and inside of the body. The outside of the body is brown felt.

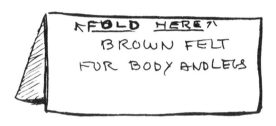

PATTERN: Take a piece of paper that is twice the height of the anteater's body and legs and as wide as the length of the anteater's body. Now fold this paper pattern in half so it is the height of the body and legs and the length of the body.

Draw the body and 4 legs. Trace pattern onto brown felt. Cut it out, glue it over the sock (holding your hand inside) let it dry. Sew on black button eyes and felt ears. TAIL is two identical felt pieces glued together and sewed on the back. Your hand goes through the back under tail to move the anteater.

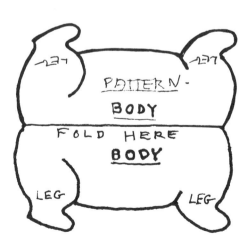

PANTYHOSE PUPPETS

TALL LADY AND TALL MAN

Each puppet is made of two pairs of solid color pantyhose that you can easily fit your hands and arms into. THE HEAD is made of two ovals with neck below made of pink felt, a size your hand will fit in. Glue on felt eyes, mouth, and nose, after you sew head pieces together around the edges. Don't sew up the neck opening. Cut a slit in back of head, insert a small flat pillow against face, and sew to hold it in place.

UPPER BODY:
Turn one pair of pantyhose upside down.
Cut hole in crotch for neck to go into. Sew it on and the head is in place. Your hand can enter through the crotch and open neck and into head behind the pillow. BODY STUFFING is another pillow sewn inside the body. The top of the lady needs one arm stuffed with polyester fiber.

125

The other arm is left as is for your own arm to go inside. The second pair of pantyhose is stuffed completely and then the top sewed to the waistband of the upper body's waistband. The second pantyhose is now the hips and legs. Cut out and finish off an open space in back of the upper body for your two hands to go inside (behind the body pillow). One hand goes inside the lady's hand and arm to move it and the other hand goes up into the head to move it. Sew on rectangle of cloth gathered at the waist as her skirt. Put beads around her neck.

THE TALL MAN
He is made the same way (without a skirt, of course), but sew a felt belt with a buckle around waist and a scarf around neck. His HEAD can be two felt profiles sewed around edges and turned inside out with felt ears glued or sewed on and finished the same way as the lady's head.

MARIONETTES (FOR CHILDREN)

PLAYMATE MARIONETTE (A CLOTH MARIONETTE)

Start by drawing paper patterns of the parts of the marionette.

HEAD and NECK: Draw and cut out the simple head and neck shapes. Trace two heads on pink felt. Cut out and sew around edges, turn inside out and stuff with polyester fiber. Sew up opening. Sew on button eyes. Felt nose and mouth are glued on. Sew on HAIR of yarn.

BODY is a rectangle-shaped pattern. Cut out two colorful cloth pieces using pattern. Sew around edges, except space left open for neck to be sewed onto body.

ARMS: They are rectangles of cloth sewn into a tube and then stuffed with polyester fiber. Sew across bend of arm. Glue two felt pink mitten shapes together as a hand. Make two. Sew onto end of arm. Sew tops of arms onto the body.

LEGS are rectangles sewed into tubes. Sew back of heel to hold up foot. Sew where leg bends, then sew onto the body.

THE CONTROLLER

It is T-shaped,
   made of light
      wood painted black.

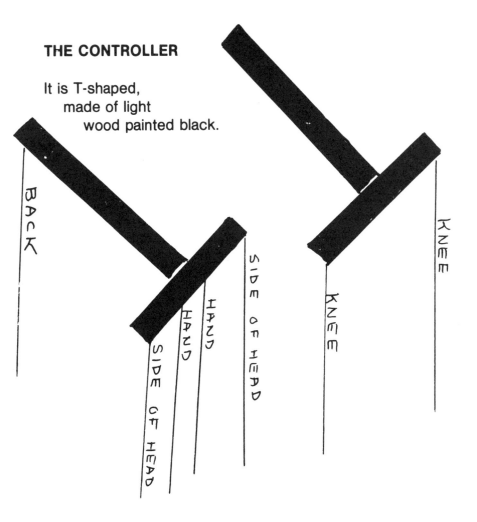

Most marionettes use two, as this one does. Strings are attached as shown in pictures. Front controller holds strings for knees. The ends of the other controller's front bar holds strings for sides of head. The hands' strings come from center of bar in front. Back end string fastens to marionette's back. Use strong black thread for marionette strings.

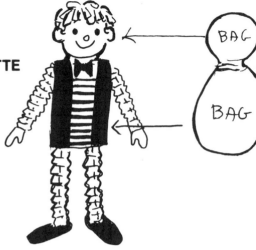

PAPER BAG MARIONETTE

HEAD: Fill one lunch bag halfway with crumpled newspapers. Paint on a face and glue on crepe paper hair.

BODY: Fill another lunch bag completely with crumpled newspapers. Put the open end of the HEAD bag inside the open end of the BODY bag. Staple the head to the body. Paint the BODY as a suit. Tie a crepe paper tie around his neck.

ARMS and LEGS: Cut a 1½-inch wide strip across the top of a package of crepe paper. Open the long crepe paper strip and sew it down the center and pull it up like a ruffle, long enough for an arm. Tie knot. Make two arms and two legs this way. Staple on body, with mitten paper hands and feet stapled on also. (Use strings just described.)

TUBE MARIONETTE

BODY: Take one cardboard tube from a roll of paper towels. Paint the tube a bright color.

130

ARMS and LEGS: Make paper chains of many strips of colorful paper. Make the lengths that look best for arms and legs.

Cut two holes in the tube for the arms and two more holes for the legs. Run one pipe cleaner through the armholes and fasten the ends that stick out around the ends of the arm chains. Then run another pipe cleaner through the leg-holes in the tube and fasten the ends of pipe cleaners to the two leg chains. Cut out two mitten paper hands and staple to the arm chains. Cut out two paper feet and staple ends of leg chains to the centers of the feet.

HEAD

THE HEAD: Cut out a paper rectangle and glue it together to make a tube. Place head tube over body tube. Glue head in back to body tube so head sticks out. Paint on a face.

HAIR: Glue on crepe paper hair. Glue on ears of paper. THE CONTROLLER operates with strings the same way as with the cloth marionette except a back string is not used.

MILK CARTON MARIONETTE

HEAD: Fold pink crepe paper 17 inches by 5 inches in half. (8½ inches by 5 inches). Put facial tissues inside and staple the two ends together, making head ready to glue sides along the edges. Draw and color eyes, nose and mouth on white paper. Cut them out and glue on the face. Add crepe paper hair.

BODY: Open up the top of an empty one-quart milk carton. Put the neck part of head way into open top of milk carton. Close top and staple it in place. Cut out a 10 by 11½-inch piece of crepe paper, then glue it onto milk-carton body.

132

LEGS: Cut out two crepe paper legs 7 by 4 inches. Glue each into a tube leg. Stuff with facial tissues. Staple across heel to hold up feet. Glue toes closed. Glue tops of legs onto carton in front.

ARMS: Cut out two 4-inch squares of crepe paper. Glue each into a tube shape. Glue on paper mitten-shaped hands. Then glue tops of arms onto sides of milk carton. Arms are stuffed with facial tissues. (Staple on hands if you wish.)

THE CONTROLLER: Fasten the strings the same way as with PLAYMATE MARIONETTE, but don't use a back string.

FUNNY BIRD MARIONETTE

BODY: Fold a nine-inch square of crepe paper in half; then round off the corners with scissors. The body is now 9 inches long and 4½ inches wide. Stuff it and glue it together.

HEAD: Draw and color the head of a bird on heavy paper. Cut it out then staple a fringe of crepe paper on top of its head. Staple head to neck.

NECK: Cut through a package of crepe paper, a strip a little over 1 inch wide. Open up the strip and sew down the center of it. As you sew pull it up into a ruffle, 7 inches long. Tie a knot. Staple onto body. Cut.

LEGS: Make ruffles like neck, but make them 5 inches long. Add paper feet stapled on.

WINGS: Cut out two crepe paper rectangles. Cut a fringe on each end. Staple them on bird as wings. Use one CONTROLLER, backwards, as seen in picture.

MY PET DRAGON

BODY: Paint one empty egg carton green.
BACK AND WING PIECES: Cut out two paper wings and a cardboard back piece. See above. Paint it.

134

Staple the wings to the back piece. Then cut a slit between the rows of eggs, lengthwise. Push the bottom of the piece through the slit. Cut out, color head and tail. Tape each inside to hold in place. They go into slits on the ends.

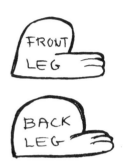

LEGS: Cut out and paint 4 cardboard legs. They are even with bottom of box when you glue them on.

AN EASY CONTROLLER for a child to make

Hook the top two hangers together. Tape them securely together. Tie a string to each X end, then onto the dragon strings. See illustration.

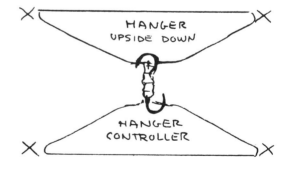

NOTE:
   Marionettes on Stage by Leonard Suib and Muriel Broadman (Harper & Row) is a marvelous book to study.

"I'M A PUPPET" (A CHILD CAN WEAR)

ROOF is painted cardboard. It's folded flat over the head area with a wide, heavy ribbon that goes through two places on the top and ties under the child's chin inside the roof. The rest of the roof is folded down on each side. Cut holes to see and breathe. Make the house like a sandwich board or a cardboard carton turned upside down  can be used. Closed part on top has a hole cut in it for the child's head to come through and holes for arms to come out. Bottom is open for the legs to be free to walk. Roof can be attached to the house if it is difficult for the child to wear it. Paint and decorate the house. Children love to put boxes on their heads, so have fun with this.

HAPPY and SAD PUPPET

THE HEAD: It is made out of a paper bag. Cut out two pieces of white paper the size of the front of the bag. Paint a HAPPY FACE on one piece of paper and a SAD FACE on the other. Glue the happy face on the front of the bag and the sad face on the back of the bag. Glue crepe paper fringe for hair on the closed top of bag and on each side. Cut out small holes to see and breathe.

BODY: Turn a cardboard box upside down. Paint and decorate it. Cut a hole for head to come through and two holes for the arms to come out.

TREE PUPPET

THE TREE TOP: Use one shopping bag. The folded side areas will now become the front and back, so flatten out the bag this new way, with the closed bottom of bag now becoming the top. Flatten out the closed top area and staple it across the top to give it a rounded look.

138

The two handles are at the bottom for the child to put his arms through to hold on the tree top. Cover the shopping bag with green crepe paper leaves glued on. Draw and paint two eyes, a nose and a mouth on white paper, cut them out and glue onto tree top to make a face with a personality. Cut holes to see and to breathe. The child wears a brown shirt and pants as a tree.

ROBOT

HEAD: Make a tube head out of heavy paper by stapling the sides together. Paint on the robot features. Glue on ears or any added parts you want him to have. Cut small holes to see and breathe.

THE BODY: Turn a cardboard carton upside down and glue paper on it. Paint on designs of mechanical parts that you imagine him to own.

Cut a hole in the closed top for the child's head to come through and a hole on each side for the arms to come out. The bottom is left open so the child can walk freely about. Tape on head when used.

A BUNNY

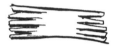

HEAD: Make a white paper tube from a rectangle of heavy paper. Staple together. Staple on white paper ears colored pink in the centers. Paint on eyes, nose and a mouth. Don't forget to cut holes to see and breathe.

WHISKERS: Cut out a rectangle of white paper. Cut a fringe on each end. Twist it in the center and glue under the nose.

BODY: Make like robot body, except paint it like a jacket. Glue cotton to the back as a tail. He would be just right for an Easter play.

TWELVE HAND-HELD STAGES (WITH GAMES TO PLAY)

(1) A PAPER BAG

Your arm goes through a HOLE you cut in the back of a paper bag. An ELF hand puppet jumps out of the open top of the bag. The elf is handed a message to read which describes a stunt the first child in line must perform. After performing, this child now holds the elf puppet, which again hops out of the bag with a new stunt for the next child. Repeat until all have had a turn.

(2) A GIFT BOX

Cut a hole in the back of a gift box for your arm to reach inside. The top of the box is open. Fill the box with stick puppet toys the children make. Before playing the game, show all of the stick puppet toys to the children. Then start by reaching through the hole in back.

Pick up a toy, but keep it out of sight. The children try to guess what toy will pop out of the box. Give hints if necessary. When a child guesses the toy you hold, then pop the toy out of the box. The child who guesses the right toy now takes your place to be the new puppeteer.

Repeat as often as you like. (Stick puppets are flat paper cutouts like a paper doll with a cardboard handle stapled on back.)

(3) A PURSE

Cut out a hole in the BACK of a discarded lady's purse. Slip your arm through the hole to hold a DOG hand puppet, which appears to be sitting in the open top of the purse. The children hide their eyes while the dog's rubber bone is hidden somewhere in the room. The children then start to look for the bone. The dog barks loudly when children get close to the bone and barks softly when far away from the bone. The child who finds it holds the dog puppet to repeat the game as often as desired.

(4) JACK IN THE BOX (OR IS IT JILL?)

Cut a hole in the back of a box. Tape a flat lid to the back so that it can easily be pushed up and down by a cardboard Jack and a cardboard Jill stick puppet.

The children line up. The puppeteer reaches in through the hole in back and picks up Jack or Jill. The first child in line guesses which puppet he thinks will pop out of the box. Then the puppeteer pushes up the puppet he was already holding before asking the question. If the child guesses the right puppet, he stays in the game. If he guesses wrong he has to sit down and leave the game. The winner is the last child left standing.

(5) BABY IN A BLANKET

Use a BABY HAND PUPPET or an old doll you can make into a hand puppet.

Drape a blanket over it and place a piece of paper inside of the blanket with the baby's future profession written on it. All of the children try to guess what the baby will be when he grows up. He makes HAPPY sounds if the children are close to the right answer and ANGRY sounds if they are wrong. Whoever guesses correctly gets to hold the baby with a new profession written on paper and put in the blanket as the game is repeated.

I HAVE A LETTER D.
WHAT TOY STARTS WITH LETTER D?
YES DOLL IS IT.

ARM

(6) A CHRISTMAS STOCKING

A puppet holds a Christmas stocking stitched to the puppet's sleeve. The stocking is filled with letters of the alphabet. The children step up one at a time. The puppet picks out a subject. The child reaches into the stocking and pulls out a letter and must immediately name an object that starts with the letter he pulls out. Example: if the puppet's subject is TOYS and the child pulls out the letter D, the child can say "DOLL" as his answer.

If the child can't give a quick answer, he must sit down and leave the game. Then the game is repeated with a new subject. Continue playing until one child remains standing.

(7) MY GARDEN

Cut out all kinds
of flowers
from a catalog.
Tell the children
the name of each
flower. Mount each flower
and staple a green colored pipe cleaner stem on back. Print names of flowers on the backs. All flowers are placed in the lid of a box (decorate to look like a picket fence). Also color and cut out a lady gardener. Staple a cardboard stick on back to hold her. TWO TEAMS PLAY. A puppeteer holds the gardener who points to a flower which the puppeteer picks up and shows to the teams. The first to guess the name wins it for his team. Guess all flowers. The team who gets the most flowers wins the game. It's educational.

(8) CUP AND SAUCER

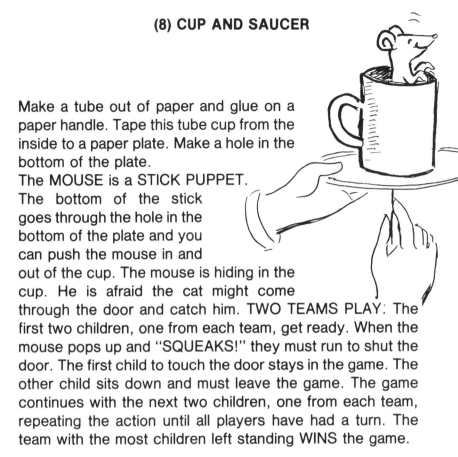

Make a tube out of paper and glue on a paper handle. Tape this tube cup from the inside to a paper plate. Make a hole in the bottom of the plate.
The MOUSE is a STICK PUPPET. The bottom of the stick goes through the hole in the bottom of the plate and you can push the mouse in and out of the cup. The mouse is hiding in the cup. He is afraid the cat might come through the door and catch him. TWO TEAMS PLAY: The first two children, one from each team, get ready. When the mouse pops up and "SQUEAKS!" they must run to shut the door. The first child to touch the door stays in the game. The other child sits down and must leave the game. The game continues with the next two children, one from each team, repeating the action until all players have had a turn. The team with the most children left standing WINS the game.

(9) CEREAL BOX

Use a large, empty cereal box. Cut a hole in back large enough for your arm to go inside to hold the ELF hand puppet.

Behind the box have a pile of pictures of FOOD the children have been shown and the main vitamins of each discussed. Give the ELF a food picture. He then holds it for two chosen teams to see. The first child to name the main vitamin content of that food WINS that picture for his team. Repeat this with each food item until all are used. Count up the pictures taken by each team to see who has the highest score.

(10) A BOOK AS A HAND-HELD STAGE

All of the children secretly make a MITT or STICK PUPPET of a favorite fairy tale or storybook character everyone knows. Keep them hidden at their desks. Each child gets a chance to sit at a table behind an upright held book with his puppet hidden behind the book. The child gives hints about his character and story until someone guesses who it is.

148

When someone gives the correct answer, the puppet peeks over the top of the book. Then the one who guessed correctly brings up his well-hidden puppet and hides it behind the book as the same game is repeated. Continue as long as you wish.

(11) A LADY'S HAT

A hole is cut out of the back of a lady's discarded hat. Your arm goes through this hole to hold a doll puppet who appears to be looking out of the open crown inside. The doll asks two teams random questions about manners and etiquette. The class could spend some time studying manners and etiquette. The child who is first to answer correctly scores one point for his team. Ask about 20 questions. The team with the highest score WINS.

(12) BIRTHDAY CAKE (A PARTY IDEA)

Cover a box with crepe paper to look like a cake. Cut out crepe paper frosting and glue it on, too. Use about ten discarded toilet tissue tubes and paint them. Cut holes on top of the cake to insert the tubes (to appear as candles). Roll up slips of paper with wishes written on them.

Insert ten wishes inside of ten different tubes on the cake. One child at a time steps up and a hand puppet points to a candle. The child takes out the paper, reads it aloud, then tells what he would do if this wish really did come true. As papers are used up, put more wish papers in the candles to replace the used ones.

NOTE: This group of puppet games can give you an opportunity to practice a little VENTRILOQUISM if you like. (Practice in front of a mirror.) A helpful book to use is VENTRILOQUISM by Darryl Hutton (Sterling Publishing Co., Inc., New York).

(1) WINDOW THEATER, APARTMENT HOUSE OR PERMA-NENT DOLLHOUSE

 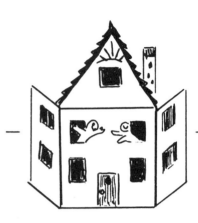

Make a house or an apartment house. It is basically built with a three-sided wood screen. Cut out the windows for the puppets to peek in and out and create a little play to perform as neighbor puppets. The back of the center part of the screen can have a few shelves which can represent floors and so the theater turns into a dollhouse or apartment house.

(2) THEATER IN A TREE

Children can create little plays from animal stories to act out in this wood tree theater or make up their own animal stories for their puppets to perform. The tree theater is also built like a three-sided hinged screen.

It is made of wood and colorfully painted. The trunk of
the tree and the space cut
out of the leaves become
the THEATER. The two
sides of the theater-like
screen become a tall fence
on each side of the tree.
The puppets can act up in
the tree theater or from
behind the fence.

(3) CASTLE THEATER

This is perfect for puppets
to act out favorite fairy
tales. The castle is cut out
and painted and
made like a
three-sided,
hinged
wood screen.

Cut out
the windows
for the puppets
to look out.
In front of the castle build another painted, three-sided, hinged wood screen to look like a lower height castle wall.

153

Puppets can act behind the wall, too, by coming out the castle door. This castle can also become a permanent castle dollhouse. On the back of the center castle wall, attach a couple of shelves to serve as floor levels in the castle. Paint interior.

CLOUD AND SPACESHIP THEATER

(4) CLOUD AND SPACESHIP THEATER

Children can act out their own science fiction space stories with rod puppets and spaceships, from behind this cloud prop, planet and spaceship theater. Cut out and paint a three-sided, hinged wood screen to look like clouds and blue sky. Then cut out a half-circle of wood and paint it to look like a planet. This half-circle planet has two wedges of wood nailed on the back so it stands up. Draw spaceship and man on heavy paper, color, cut out and staple rods on back.

BACK OF PLANET

(5) BOAT THEATER

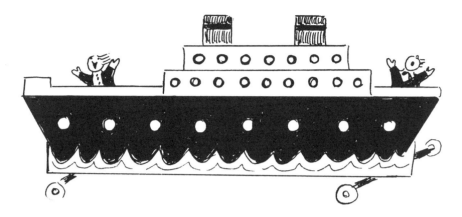

The children should study all about foreign countries they like; then their hand puppets get on the BOAT THEATER and describe in detail the wonderful vacations they expect to have.

BACK VIEW
OF BOAT PROP

When the description is completed, the puppets wave good-by and sail off stage. The boat is painted and cut out of wood. A shelf to kneel upon is nailed on the back, along with handles to hold onto when moving the boat. This shelf has four wheels which make it easy for the puppeteers kneeling on the shelf to roll the boat off the stage. One leg kneels and the other foot pushes the boat along like a scooter.

The puppeteers are hidden from the audience. Only the puppets can be seen as if in the boat.
NOTE: You will have to experiment with wheel balance or make the boat as a three-sided screen.

(6) ELEPHANT THEATER

Cut out a large wood elephant and paint him.

CAN YOU REMEMBER WHAT I TELL YOU?

Nail the elephant to a strong wooden toy box that has a strong lid. The toy box is in back of him. A child can stand on the lid and operate the puppet from there. The elephant can become a memory theater to play memory games. Since the elephant is known for his memory, he is our representative.

IDEAS TO USE TO TEST A CHILD'S MEMORY

(1) Speak a long sentence and see who can correctly repeat it.

(2) Speak short poems or rhymes. Who can repeat them?

(3) Who can correctly repeat a melody?

(4) Give directions and street numbers to reach a specific place. Who can repeat this?

(5) Who can repeat telephone numbers and area codes correctly?

(6) Show pictures of places, then see who can describe them in detail when they are put away.

(7) Have each of the children draw a picture of a fictitious person and write a name on the back of the picture. Each picture is held up and the name is given. Then see who remembers the most names by writing down the name as each picture is held up.

(8) Hold up newspaper photos of well-known people. Who can give the first and last name of each one? Also do this with historical people.
NOTE: A good memory is very important in and out of school, in fact all through a person's life. Also, school toys or supplies can be stored in the toy box behind the elephant.

(7) COUNTRY THEATER IN A BARN (OR SUMMER STOCK THEATER)

The children write and perform their own puppet plays through the barn's half open door.

They can write plays about farm life, farm production, etc. The barn is made like a hinged three-sided wood screen cut into a barn shape and painted. This barn can also be used as a barn doll house for farm adventure play when not using it as a theater.

(8) SCHOOLHOUSE THEATER

This school can be used as a QUIZ THEATER between competing teams or in-dividuals. Use puppets to ask questions through the school windows. The quiz can be a contest in spelling, math, or any subject currently being studied.

Cut out and paint a three-sided, hinged wood screen in the shape of this schoolhouse. When not being used as a theater, it can become a quiet reading nook by a bookcase.

(9) HOUSEBOAT THEATER

This is a three-sided, hinged theater screen cut out of wood and painted to look like a HOUSEBOAT. The puppets sing songs on deck and through the houseboat windows. Also see if the children can learn a little two-part harmony. Puppets can also tell jokes or riddles. When the houseboat is not being used as a theater, it can be used as a houseboat dollhouse with a shelf attached in back as a different floor level.

(10) CAR THEATER

It is made on the same principle as the moving-boat theater. It is cut out of wood and painted with cutout windows for the puppets to look out. The back of the car has a kneeling shelf and small wheels attached through the fake wheels in front and back. The puppeteer can kneel with one leg on the shelf in back and push the car along with the other foot so that it can roll right off the stage waving good-by.

Cut out windows for the puppets to look out and tell you about the special trip they are going to take. NOTE: Experiment with the wheels for perfect balance, or make the car into a three-sided screen (nonmoving).

(11) CHRISTMAS TREE THEATER WITH GIFT BOXES

Let's have a Christmas party. Make a stylized, flat, green wood Christmas tree with boxes painted on the bottom and sides to form a three-sided, hinged screen with the flat tree in the center. Screw cup hooks all over the tree to hang ornaments on it. The puppets act out original holiday stories and sing carols from behind the boxes and tree. They can also play a hiding game with the audience. Hide toys behind the boxes and move them about to see who can guess where they moved to. Also hang up paper Christmas balls with stunts printed on back of each. Children must choose a ball and perform stunt on back.

This train is cut out of wood, and each car is nailed onto the back of a wood box (also used for storage). The children sit on the boxes with their puppets. They tell tales of adventures they pretend to have with their puppets all through America now or during historical times. Now try your own ideas. It is fun to create new things to delight children.

TWELVE PUPPET THEATERS

(HOMEMADE THEATERS THAT ARE DIFFERENT)

NOTE: These fun theaters are made like three-sided screens and from things you could have at home.

(1) TWO-BOX THEATER (OR TWO-FLAT THEATER)

Make up plays where two families can interchange ideas acted out through the upstairs and downstairs windows, up on the roof or outside behind the fence. LET'S MAKE IT: Take two cardboard cartons that are the same size and glue them together, with the open parts in the back. Cut out and glue two walls on the sides. Cut out the windows.

Make a wall for a roof garden by cutting out and glueing a cardboard strip on the edges of the roof. Cut a rectangle out of the top of the roof so the puppets appear to be on the roof in the roof garden. Paint the theater and put on a puppet show with puppets coming out the windows and puppets on the roof and looking over the wall. Lots of action!

(2) A TRAVELING GARMENT RACK THEATER

GARMENT BAG
THEATER

This is a temporary, fun SCHOOLROOM THEATER.

Take a garment rack that is sold in department stores and department store catalog order books. It has wheels to conveniently roll in and out of a room. Next, take a GARMENT BAG and hang it on the rack with the zipper side unzipped all the way and facing the BACK, where you will operate the puppets. Cut out an opening for the puppets to act in front, facing the audience. Tape the edges with colorful tape to frame it. Hang curtain pieces on the sides to finish it. Tape a sheer black curtain to the inside of the open space. Now you can reach in through the back of the bag with your puppets and perform in front of the sheer black curtain opening.

NOTE: This GARMENT RACK THEATER, when not in use as a theater, can be used to hang school costumes, etc., in for convenient storage.

3) A CARD TABLE THEATER

Open a card table and put it on its side with all four legs extending out to the back. Slip a curtain onto each side, using the top legs as curtain rods. Cut out and paint a cardboard THEATER TOP with an open space for the puppets to appear. The THEATER TOP has its front and sides. Decorate to look like a PUPPET THEATER. Clamp or clip the theater top to the curtain legs on top. Now you have a temporary theater that can be used to perform with your puppets. When finished, slip off curtains and top theater and you have a table to use again for play.

(4) THE LIVE CURTAIN THEATERS

Two children hold a rod with a curtain on it.

Puppeteers are below the curtain and reach up with their puppets to perform very short plays.

ANOTHER IDEA USING TWO CURTAINS ON RODS

This idea (see picture) uses two curtains on rods. The children in front hold the curtain a little lower this time. They sit on chairs with the curtain rod on their shoulders. The other two children stand and hold the second curtain on a rod as a backdrop for scenery, which is cut out of paper, colored and pinned with straight pins to the backdrop. The puppeteers reach up and perform in front of the backdrop with the other curtain in front of them.

(5) OUTDOOR THEATER IN THE ROUND

This theater is made with pickets on a wire fence and placed outdoors in a circle.

The children are dressed as puppets and act out plays inside this circle. They wear paper costumes that they make.

NOTE: The fence can remain as a permanent play area when not used for shows. Be sure to leave an area open in back as an entrance and an exit.

(6) ONE-CHAIR THEATER

A child puppeteer uses a pillowcase type of curtain that slips over the back of a chair. Make it of two pieces of cloth sewed around the edges like a pillowcase.

The back of the chair faces the audience. The puppeteer talks back and forth to his puppet and to his audience. It can be a fun idea for question and answer sessions on subjects studied in school. This puts fun into a quiz. Shy children find it easier to talk to a puppet.

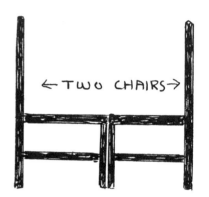

←TWO CHAIRS→

(7) TWO-CHAIR THEATER

Place two chairs together as pictured, fronts of seats together. Tape a curtain rod across the BACK TOPS of the chairs. This curtain rod holds a sheer black curtain as a back-drop. Cover the two seats with a green painted cardboard. This becomes the ground area to at-tach cardboard props of trees, bushes, houses, fences, etc. Each has a pipe cleaner shaped

CURTAINS HIDE PUPPETEERS AND LEGS OF CHAIRS

like an L stapled on back. The bottom of this L pipe cleaner is like a stand taped to the ground area to hold up each prop. Some props need two stands attached.

Use stick puppets with L-shaped pipe cleaner handles stapled on the back of each to move them about the stage in front of the black sheer curtain that the puppeteer can see through as he works. Also attach curtains around the legs, front and sides of the chairs. This hides the puppeteer. Make different paper stick puppets to change often.

(8) WALKING-BOX THEATER

Use an empty cardboard carton, big enough for a child to wear. Cut out a circle for his head to go through and a rectangle in front of the circle for his hands to go through to hold the puppets. See illustration. Paint and decorate the box.
HEAD PIECE: The scenery is painted on white paper and is glued to the flat side of a paper bag that is worn on the puppeteer's head as a backdrop. Tape it temporarily to the box when in use. Be sure to cut small holes for puppeteer to see and to breathe. He is now a walking theater.

(9) A BOOKCASE PUPPET THEATER

The children act with their puppets behind a bookcase that is near a wall. They paint a scene on a large sheet of paper and use it as a backdrop for the puppet play. The scene is taped to the wall behind the bookcase for the puppets to act in front of it.

(10) A CLOTHESLINE THEATER (SUMMER FUN)

Cut out a rectangular shape in a discarded sheet.

Attach colorful tape around the edges to give this open space a colorful finish. Fasten the top of the sheet securely to the clothesline with clip clothespins. Secure the bottom corners to ground stakes in your yard to keep it in place. Now the puppets will be able to act out a puppet show from behind the open cutout space.

(11) PICNIC TABLE PUPPET THEATER

This is fun if you plan a backyard picnic party for children.

Move your picnic table right in front of your clothesline.

Hang a sheet or cloth on your clothes-line and clip it on with clothespins. Then paint large colorful trees, bushes, a fence, house, etc., on white paper, cut out and attach to the sheet with safety pins from the back. Cover picnic table with a large tablecloth. Then the puppeteers hide behind the table and reach up with the puppets to perform in front of the colorful background.

(12) A SHOPPING BAG THEATER

Take a shopping bag and cut out an opening in the back. Front: Cut open like shutters, folded back. Puppets go through the back and look out the front to perform. Decorate bag or cover with Con-Tact paper, etc.

171

172

PUPPETS DRAW TEN RIDDLES

The puppets draw the question pictures and the answer pictures with chalk on the chalkboard or with a marker on a large demonstration pad of paper. The puppet asks the riddle and if the audience doesn't know the answer, the puppet draws the answer. Puppets best to use are those which can draw with a chalk or marker held in its mouth. If too hard to do, you draw and the puppet asks questions. The puppets draw with mouth, elephant trunk or hand, which is your hand in glove hand of puppet.

RIDDLES

(1) QUESTION: "What has a roof and never a wall?"

ANSWER: "An umbrella."

(2) QUESTION: "What does your nose know?"

ANSWER: "When it's time to eat."

(3) QUESTION: "Why is this heart lonely and sad?"

ANSWER: "It needs a heart to make it glad."

(4) QUESTION: "It POPS! It's on my nose or shoe. What stays where you don't want it to?"

QUESTION

ANSWER: "You chew and chew, you're never through with chewing gum you love to chew."

ANSWER

(5) QUESTION: "When is a board half asleep?"

ANSWER: "When it's bored."

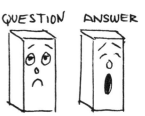
QUESTION   ANSWER

(6) QUESTION: "When does a fan look like a tail?"

QUESTION

ANSWER: "When it's a fantail."
ANSWER

(7) QUESTION: "What can children never stop?"

QUESTION ?

ANSWER

ANSWER: "Growing up to reach their top!"

MORE RIDDLES ON THE NEXT PAGE......

174

(8) QUESTION: "What do we like that is full of holes?"

QUESTION

ANSWER: "DOUGHNUTS."

ANSWER

(9) QUESTION: "When can a string stand up and fly?"

ANSWER: "When tied to a balloon that escapes in the sky."

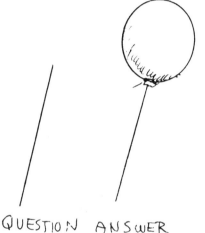

QUESTION   ANSWER

(10) QUESTION: "Who robbed the bank? He had 6 eyes."

QUESTION

ANSWER: "A masked man with glasses, he was one of the guys."

ANSWER

175

TEN MORE RIDDLES
ON A T-SHIRT
PARADE

Children dress up as "ME" PUP-PETS: They wear paper tube heads and sandwich board T-shirts made of card-board with the question and pic-ture on the front and the answer and its picture on the back. The narrator reads the question on the T-shirt as each of ten children parade before the audience. If the audience can't guess the riddle, the puppet child turns around to show the answer on the back and the narrator tells the answer, too. The TUBE HEAD each child wears is a rectangle of paper with its ends stapled together. Draw and paint on a face. Glue on a nose, ears and crepe paper hair. THE T-SHIRT is two cardboard pieces with the question and answer on them. A broad rib-bon tape is stapled at the top on each side. The two ribbon tapes rest on the shoulders to hold on the T-shirt. See pic-ture.

RIDDLES

(1) QUESTION: "Why happy smiles and running feet?"

ANSWER: "It's time for lunch, let's go, let's eat."

(2) QUESTION: "What can scratch, what can clean?"

ANSWER: "A witch's broom on Halloween!"

(3) QUESTION: "When are you flat, and still you look round? You can't answer that. You can't make a sound."

ANSWER: "When you're a picture."

(4) QUESTION: "What has a bark you can not hear?"

ANSWER: "A tree."

(5) QUESTION: "What acts like you that you can't chase away?"

ANSWER: "Your shadow."

(6) QUESTION: "What can you give that will be given back to you?"

ANSWER: "Give someone a smile and they'll give you one,too."

(7) QUESTION: "Some windows go up.....some windows go down. What kind of windows move all around?"

ANSWER: "Cars, trucks, planes, etc."

(8) QUESTION: "Who must walk on the street but not on the sidewalk?"

ANSWER: "A parade of people."

(9) QUESTION: "What tiny creatures can move a house?"

ANSWER: "Turtles and snails (their houses are their shells)."

(10) QUESTION: "When are we in two places at the same time?"

ANSWER: "When we are asleep in our bed and dream we are in some other place."

180

PUPPETS DRAW CHALK TALKS

Puppets holds chalk in mouth to draw on chalkboard as poem is recited. Follow numbers, or use felt tip pen on paper. If you prefer, puppet speaks and you draw the picture.

POEM

(1) Do you like this little letter c?
I think it's just too small.

(2) Let's make it big, then bigger still.

(3) Now you see, the C can crawl.
(What is it? Answer: A SNAIL.)

DRAWING DIRECTIONS: (for POEM)

(1) Draw a small letter c.

(2) Circle the small letter
into a bigger letter c like this:

(3) Complete the snail as shown.

CHALK TALK POEM

THE IGLOO

(1) In the far away land of the Eskimo,
     In the igloo safe and sound.
(2) The igloo is safe the Eskimo found,
     When a polar bear comes around.

DRAW AS YOU RECITE POEM, MATCH NUMBERS.

(1) Draw the igloo.

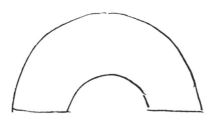

(2) Turn the igloo into a polar bear as you draw.

CHALK TALK POEM

OH, WHERE IS THE PEAR?

(1) A pear upon a table sat
      Then someone knocked it over.
(2) A little boy stood by and cried,
      "The pear's inside of Rover!"

DRAW AS YOU RECITE POEM, MATCH NUMBERS.

(1) Draw a PEAR. Use paper and pen.

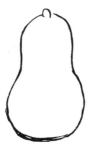

(2) Turn pear on its side and turn it into the dog Rover as you draw.

CHALK TALK POEM

PEANUTS?

(1) Why do these peanuts stand on the floor?
    Because they're not peanuts. Then what are they for?

(2) They are part of a picture that purrrs a "meow."
    So I'll finish the picture....What do I have now?"
    (Answer) A mother cat with kittens.

DRAW AS YOU RECITE POEM, MATCH NUMBERS.

(1) Draw these four PEANUTS.

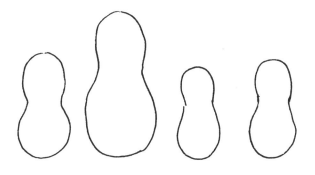

(2) Draw faces as cat and kittens. Add legs and tails, etc.

PUPPETS DRAW FOUR GAMES

WHERE DOES JOHNNY LIVE?

A puppet with a felt tip pen in his mouth draws a building and lots of windows on a large piece of paper clipped onto an easel. The children hide their eyes as the puppeteer draws an X on the back of the large picture behind one of the windows. Then one child at a time comes up and writes an X and his/her first name next to the X mark. After all of the children do this, the puppeteer lifts up the paper and pushes a PIN through the X he made on BACK of the picture. The child who has his X closest to the PINPOINT wins the picture because he guessed where Johnny lives in the building.

THE HAUNTED HOUSE

(TEAM GAME)

A puppet holds a felt tip pen in his mouth and draws a rickety old house on a large piece of paper clipped onto an easel.

Two TEAMS of children hide their eyes. The puppeteer takes the picture from the easel and writes twenty different numbers on the back behind different parts of the house.

187

This is where the money is hidden for the children to find. When he clips the picture back on the board, the numbers on the back can't be seen. One child at a time (alternating from each team) draws a small X and writes his name with small letters next to his X mark. When all of the children finish, someone writes down the team's scores while the puppeteer pushes the pin through each number on the back. The number is given to the child whose X is closest to the pinpoint called. He wins the number to be added to his team's score. After all numbers have been pinpointed, each team's score is added to see which team wins the picture. The child with the largest number on a team takes the picture home.

A FLEA ON A DOG, WHERE IS IT?

A puppet draws a funny dog's head
with a felt tip pen in the puppet's mouth.
Make this a large dog head on a large piece
of paper clipped onto an easel. Then all of the
children hide their eyes as the puppeteer draws an X on the back of the picture where a FLEA is hiding. Hang the picture up again and have each child draw a small X and place his name somewhere on the front of the picture.

When all of the children have their names and X marks finished, the puppeteer pushes a pin through the flea on the back.
The child with his X closest to the pinpoint wins the dog picture as his prize.

A WOODPECKER IN A TREE.

WHERE IS HE?

A puppet with a felt tip pen in his
mouth draws a tree on a large piece
of paper on an easel. The children hide
their eyes as the puppeteer draws an X on
back of the picture to show where the
WOODPECKER is hiding. Then each child comes
up, draws an X and places his name on the front where he
thinks the woodpecker hides in the tree. The puppeteer
then pushes a pin through the X where the bird hides in
BACK. The child whose X mark is closest to the X pinpoint in
the tree wins the picture to take home.
NOTE: If it is too difficult to draw with the puppet, YOU do
the drawing while the puppet speaks to the children.

SIX MINI PLAYS FOR PUPPETS

SIX MINIPLAYS FOR PUPPETS

THE BIG BALLOON ACTIONS THAT GO WITH POEM

MATCH these ACTION NUMBERS to the POEM NUMBERS for play.

CHARACTERS IN PLAY:

BALLOON MAN   HUNGRY BIRD
BALLOON   BIG CLOUD
KITE   BOY

(1)
ACTION: Balloon man moves about stage.

(2)
Make the BALLOON MAN move down, so it appears that the BALLOON is floating up. Clouds on rods move behind balloon.

(3)
Sad face of BALLOON shows as more clouds on rods float behind him.

(4)
The clouds float lower and disappear leaving the BALLOON all alone.

(5)
A KITE floats in and BALLOON'S smile side shows.

THE BIG BALLOON PUPPET PLAY
(Poem)

(1)
Balloons are seen just everywhere,
    In a park or zoo.
A man who sold them smiled and said,
    "Come take one home with you."

(2)
Then suddenly a big balloon
    He thought was held quite tight,
Had slipped right from his fingers.
    Up to the sky in flight.

(3)
The big balloon looked down below
    And gave a little sigh,
"Now who can buy this poor balloon
    Which is floating in the sky?"

(4)
The big balloon kept going up
    As high as you could see.
"By night," it cried, "I'll pass the moon;
    What will become of me?"

(5)
Quite suddenly a kite said, "Hi.
    Come tie your string to mine!
Then we can go back down to earth."
    The plan they thought was fine.

THE BIG BALLOON ACTIONS THAT GO WITH POEM

(6) KITE flees as a big bird appears chasing sad-faced balloon back and forth.

(7) A big cloud comes and the BALLOON goes behind it. The BIRD looks angrily about, gives up and flies away.

(8) Make the cloud go up and down and finally out of sight. (Sad BALLOON alone.)

(9) Make a wind sound. The sad BALLOON blows all about.

(10) The house prop comes up from below so it appears the BALLOON is moving down.

BIG BALLOON PUPPET PLAY
(Poem)

(6)
But then a great big hungry bird
 Pecked at the big balloon.
"Oh dear, if this balloon should POP,
 "Its end would come too soon!"

(7)
A great big cloud then came along
 and offered it a ride.
The big balloon crawled in to hide
 So soft and safe inside.

(8)
They floated on, but when the cloud
 Began to disappear,
The big balloon looked down below,
 Saw hills and houses near.

(9)
A windy, windy wind began to
 Blow across the sky.
It blew the big balloon about
 And it began to cry.
It went DOWN, DOWN, DOWN!

(10)
The big balloon then struck a HOUSE!
 "Oh dear, I mustn't POP!"
And there it stayed right where it was,
 Beneath a high rooftop.

(11)
Boy pulls balloon inside from behind the side of the house.
Balloon smiles.

(12)
Boy and balloon peek out smiling from behind the side of the
house.

(11)
"But who will see me way up here?"
    A window opened wide,
A BOY HAD SEEN A STRING HANG DOWN
    SOOOOOOOOOOOO ....

(12)
    The balloon was pulled inside.
The big balloon now had a home,
    "I'm happy, safe and sound;
I thought I had no home at all,
    Once lost, but now I'm found."

CURTAIN

PRODUCTION NOTES:

Make STICK PUPPETS and PROPS that you attach to rods
that are painted the color blue, like the sky, where most of
these story poems take place. THE BALLOON is made of
two firm pieces of paper glued together with the rod inside.
The BALLOON has a SAD FACE painted on one side and a
HAPPY FACE painted on the other side. When you want to
change faces, either twirl the balloon slightly or have it move
quickly in and out of sight while you change the face. All the
other PROPS are single-faced as props or characters.

The bird can have a wing on a paper fastener and the rod can move up and down to fly the bird. The kite tail can be wired to stand out. The house is pushed up from below and clamped just behind the inside front of the stage. The BALLOON and boy move in and out behind the side, appearing to be going in and peeking out of a side window of the house.

THE BIRTHDAY PARTY (MINIPLAY)

THE STAGE SETTING

MISSY'S DINING ROOM

CHARACTERS:
 MISSY
 SUSAN
 MIKE
 BILLY
 CAROL
 TIM
 SHAG (HE IS A PUPPET.)
SEE PRODUCTION NOTES.

ALL ARE
LIVE CHILDREN.

SHAG, THE DOG

THE PLAY:

The scene takes place in MISSY'S
DINING ROOM.
She is sitting by a large dining room table with four chairs.
She is crying, and her dog SHAG tries to comfort her.

MISSY: Nobody likes me because I'm the new girl in the neighborhood. Today is my BIRTHDAY! I know I won't have a birthday party THIS year! Nobody even knows I'm alive! (She puts her head down and cries some more. Suddenly, she stops and listens. She stands up and looks around.)

MISSY: I hear voices! I hear children singing outside!
SHAG barks (and runs through the door to the living room).
CHILDREN'S voices singing off stage:

HAPPY BIRTHDAY to you, HAPPY BIRTHDAY to you, HAPPY BIRTHDAY to you..... (Missy turns and looks surprised as Susan walks in through the living room door with a big birthday cake and candles, and she is followed by her classmates: Mike, Billy, Carol, and Tim. They are carrying big birthday presents and still singing the BIRTHDAY SONG. Susan sets the big birthday cake on the table and they all cry out SURPRISE! Missy claps her hands joyfully.)

SUSAN: Miss Joyce, our teacher, told us YOU had a birthday and we want to WELCOME YOU to the neighborhood! (MISSY hugs Susan.)

MISSY: Thank you, thank you, EVERYBODY! Mike, Billy, Carol, Tim and Susan. Such a beautiful BIRTHDAY CAKE!
(Shag enters with a happy BARK, and everybody laughs.)
THE CHILDREN IN UNISON SAY: Missy, OPEN your BIRTHDAY PRESENTS! (Missy smiles as Mike gives her HIS present.)

MIKE: Can you guess what is inside?

MISSY (turns to the audience and says): No, but there are children here to help me. CHILDREN IN THE AUDIENCE, HELP ME.

(MISSY peeks behind the PICTURE birthday box. The FRONT OF EACH FLAT PRETEND BOX HAS GIFT WRAPPING PAINTED ON IT and the BACK of the FLAT PICTURE BOX has the GIFT PAINTED ON IT. A few children in the audience try to guess what is "in" the PACKAGE.)

MISSY: I've opened my present, and now I'll show you....IT'S A DOLL! (She turns the picture gift around so the audience sees it.)

MISSY: Oh, thank you, Mike, I LOVE my doll. I'll put her right over here. (Missy leans it against the table for everyone to see.)
BILLY (steps up and hands Missy HIS present): I'll bet you can't guess what THIS is!

MISSY: Oh, thank you, Billy. I can't wait to open this, but first I want the children to guess again. (Missy peeks at the back of the present to see if anyone guesses what is inside. A few children try.)

MISSY: Now I'll show you my present. (She turns the present around to show the audience.) It's a JAR OF LOLLIPOPS! Mmmmmmmm, they look DELICIOUS! We'll all have one, or two...thank you, Billy, we'll share these. (Missy stands the gift in front of the table.)

(CAROL steps up and gives Missy HER present.)

MISSY: This is going to be FUN! Oh, thank you, Carol, I wonder what is inside? (She shakes the box back and forth and looks on the back and smiles.)

MISSY: Audience, guess what Carol brought me. (The audience guesses a few times.)

MISSY: It's a BEAUTIFUL red sweater! My FAVORITE color and just what I need for school. Thank you so much, Carol. (Missy stands this present against the table for all to see.) (Tim steps up to give Missy HIS present.)

TIM: This is something practical, Missy. Hope you like it.

MISSY: Thank you, Tim. Now I am really CURIOUS to know what THIS present is.   Audience, HELP me! (The audience tries to guess as Missy peeks at the picture gift on the back. Missy turns the picture around for the audience to see.)

MISSY: Look! How WONDERFUL. Miss Joyce, our teacher, will be delighted! Tim, you gave me SCHOOL SUPPLIES!

Pencils, pens, paper, notebooks, scissors, crayons, EVERYTHING, and Susan, thank you again for the beautiful BIRTHDAY CAKE. We can ALL have some!
(Shag BARKS, and Missy looks out the window.)

MISSY: Look, Mother has made sandwiches and cold punch to go with our BIRTHDAY CAKE. Let's all go out onto the patio and have our BIRTHDAY PARTY.

(Missy picks up her BIRTHDAY CAKE and all the children follow her out the living room door. Shag stays behind and watches. Then he turns and faces the audience and sings some of the BIRTHDAY song in a barking voice. He ends with a real bark, and scampers out the same door to join the children on the patio.)

CURTAIN

PRODUCTION NOTES:

SHAG is the ONLY PUPPET in this play. This is how to make him: Take some white paper wide enough to go around the head of the child who plays the part of the dog, SHAG. Staple the HEAD into a TUBE shape that easily fits over the head of the child.

Form another tube shape for the nose. Staple the X's together and cut off the shaded area in illustration to round off the end of the nose on both sides. Turn up the opposite side a little to glue onto the head. Now you have the basis for the head. Cut small spaces for puppeteer to breathe and see.

Then cut white strips of crepe paper with a fringe cut on one edge. Glue these   strips all over the head and neck area, as well as on the nose, except for the end. The ears are black crepe paper. Glue on black round eyes and nose.

DOG'S BODY

Cut enough white paper to cover a child's body when kneeling down. Cover it with white fringes like the head. Staple two ribbons (or more, if needed) to tie dog's body around child's waist. Glue on fringed black crepe paper tail and red felt collar.

THE BIRTHDAY PRESENTS

They are just a square or rectangular piece of white cardboard. Paint a ribbon and bow on one side and on the other side paint the gift image.

BIRTHDAY CAKE

Paint it
on cardboard.
Cut it out.
Then on the back
glue two right angle pieces.
STAGE SETTING is a dining room. It has a table and four chairs and an open door. A fake window is painted on cardboard and put up and a rug is placed on the floor. A picture can hang on the wall for balance.

VALENTINES (A HAND PUPPET PLAY)

(All voices can be recorded and played on tape as puppets perform.)

CHARACTERS:
 GRETCHEN
 CHRIS
 PILOT

TIME:
A time in
FEBRUARY.

SETTING: Chris and Gretchen's California backyard.

THE PLAY

NARRATOR: (offstage) Here we are in California. See that little girl sitting out in her backyard? She is writing Valentine letters to her pen pals. Her brother Chris is busy inside of the house. He is writing Valentine letters, too.
Let's watch and listen.
GRETCHEN: We have been writing Valentine letters all morning to our pen pals. They can't get out to play. We must be sure to make Valentines for every one of them. (Chris runs out of the house to join Gretchen.)
CHRIS: I am almost through with mine.

I sent Valentine letters to New York, Chicago, Des Moines, San Francisco, Los Angeles; name any place and I'll bet I wrote to someone there.

GRETCHEN: Let's take them inside and put them in our LETTER BASKET so that we can mail them. (Gretchen brushes them off of the table toward the back to give the illusion they are falling into a bag which she picks up behind the table and carries into the house.)

NARRATOR: The children went inside. Here they come out again with their basketful of Valentine letters. Suddenly a wind howls! It is really blowing! Come on audience, make howling WIND sounds. Gretchen drops her basket.
(The puppeteer below tosses up letters to appear they are blowing. Chris and Gretchen run back and forth making actions of picking up letters. The wind sound stops! The puppeteer below puts letters back into the basket. Gretchen reaches down and picks up basketful of Valentine letters again. It looks as though the children filled the basket.)

GRETCHEN: I hope that we found all of the letters.

CHRIS: No one must be disappointed on Valentine's Day.

GRETCHEN: Let's hurry to the post office and mail them. (The children run off with the Valentine basket.)

NARRATOR: It is near the end of February. The children are now coming out of their house. They are still concerned about the Valentines.

CHRIS: So MANY DAYS have passed.

GRETCHEN: Do you think Linda received her Valentine?

CHRIS: How about Pete or Sandy or Tim?

GRETCHEN: Listen, I hear a loud sound. what can it be?

CHRIS: It's up in the sky. LOOK! (Chris points to the sky.)

GRETCHEN: It's a HELICOPTER with red hearts painted all over it. (This is a single piece of cardboard with a helicopter painted on it. The helicopter has a ledge with paper hearts on it. When the puppeteer tips the helicopter the hearts slide off and fall below, or have the helicopter partially disappear with a puppeteer tossing down the hearts giving the illusion they came from the helicopter.)

PILOT calls out: Hey down there! These Valentines are from all of the boys and girls you wrote to. They are for CHRIS and GRETCHEN. (They hop up and down and exclaim): Oh thank you, again and again! There are VALENTINES from EVERYONE!

CHRIS: Our Valentine's Day lasted all month long!

GRETCHEN: It's the best Valentine's Day we ever had! CHRIS and GRETCHEN: Happy Valentine's Day to EVERYONE!!!

CURTAIN

PRODUCTION NOTES:

The BACKDROP has the fence, tree, and sky painted on it. A cardboard HOUSE is painted and cut out. Also paint and cut out a cardboard table. Both single-faced PROPS are attached just INSIDE the front of the stage. The puppets can work behind the house as they pretend to go inside and outside again.

THE KING AND QUEEN OF EASTER EGG HILL

(Use hand puppets. Voices are taped to use as puppets perform.)

CHARACTERS:

SHARON
EASTER BUNNY
A BUNNY HELPER
BUD AND JAKE, mischievous BOYS
SUSY FLOWER in a pot who narrates from the windowsill

TIME: Morning before Easter.

SETTING: BOBBY and SHARON'S backyard.

BOBBY AND SHARON'S YARD

EASTER EGG HILL

THE PLAY

SUSY FLOWER (puppet on the windowsill): Hi! It's me, Susy Flower. Look on the windowsill! People don't really expect a flower to talk to them, do they? Well, let me tell you. There will be a brand new EASTER BUNNY coming to visit this year. This new Easter Bunny is very young and wants to be sure to make a good impression on everyone. He hid eggs all over the yard. Here he comes, hopping up the path.....

(Susy Flower looks around.) I'll be quiet and watch him. (The EASTER BUNNY knocks on the door. BOBBY and SHARON come out of the house and see him.)

BOBBY: Easter Bunny! We have NEVER seen YOU before!

EASTER BUNNY: I know; I'm new at this sort of thing. I just hid Easter eggs for you to find, all over your backyard! (Two mischievous boys look over the fence.)

MISCHIEVOUS BUD: We know where they are; we watched when the Easter Bunny hid them.

JAKE: We TOOK them ALL for ourselves. You can't have ANY! (The mischievous boys laugh and run away. Sharon and Bobby cry!)

EASTER BUNNY: Don't cry. I will come back right away with something beautiful for you.
(The BUNNY hops down the path and disappears.)

SHARON: I wonder what the EASTER BUNNY will bring us?

BOBBY: Look! He's coming back with Easter hats!

SHARON: Oh, BEAUTIFUL hats, how wonderful we will look in them. (Easter Bunny appears, hopping up the path with the hats. Sharon hugs him.)

SHARON: Oh, thank you. They are BEAUTIFUL!

SHARON (smiling): So fancy, too! (Bud and Jake look over the fence again and laugh sarcastically.)

BUD: If you wear THOSE, we'll make sure EVERYONE in town LAUGHS at you and your SILLY HATS!

JAKE: (jeering): No one wears RIDICULOUS HATS anymore! (They both laugh and run away.)

SUSY FLOWER: Bobby and Sharon put their hats down. They feel embarrassed and ashamed to wear the hats. They reluctantly give them back to the EASTER BUNNY, who is sorry, too.

EASTER BUNNY: I'll be back with something you will really like....You'll see. (The Easter Bunny hops down the path and disappears carrying the hats.)

SUSY FLOWER: Poor Bobby and Sharon and poor Easter Bunny. I can see him hopping far away and disappearing over a hill.
(Susy Flower shakes her head in a negative way.) Look! Here he comes back again. He looks HAPPY! He is carrying a basket of something new again. I wonder what it is?

EASTER BUNNY (appears hopping up the path):   I have CHOCOLATE EASTER EGGS for you, Bobby and Sharon.

BOBBY and SHARON: Oh, thank you!

(Bud and Jake come running from behind the fence.)

BUD (shouts): We want those CHOCOLATE EGGS. Those are for us! (The Easter Bunny runs away with the Easter eggs. Bud and Jake run after the Easter Bunny. Bobby and Sharon run inside of the house.)

SUSY FLOWER: WELL! The Easter Bunny got away with the chocolate eggs. I could see him disappear over the hill, and Bud and Jake FELL into a puddle of MUD! My goodness, things are QUIET now. It has been quite awhile. (Susy looks inside the window.) Sharon and Bobby are still consoling each other. (Susy looks down the path.) Oh look! Here comes the Easter Bunny! He isn't carrying ANYTHING this time. (The Easter Bunny comes up the path and knocks on the door, then hops on to the path again. Bobby and Sharon come outside to greet him.)

EASTER BUNNY: Tonight, we will build a SURPRISE for you while you are asleep. It will be all finished for you to see in the morning, Easter morning.

BOBBY and SHARON: Oh, thank you, Easter Bunny. You try so hard to make us happy. (The children go into the house.)

SUSY FLOWER: There goes the Easter Bunny, skipping happily away.

I wonder what he is planning to do?. It's beginning to get dark now, VERY DARK! (The stage light dims.) I see two bunnies coming over the hill. I see two shadowy figures of two bunnies pulling a big cart. (The two bunnies in shadow pull a shadow-like cart off of the stage to the side by the fence. It appears to be out of sight.)

SUSY FLOWER: It's the EASTER Bunny and another Bunny. I can hardly see them in the moonlight. They are building something! (The bunnies go back and forth to the side by the cart, making motions like they are picking up things and moving them into a pile.)

SUSY FLOWER: They are building something that is getting higher and higher! It is growing bigger and BIGGER! Oh, it looks like a mountain or a HILL in the backyard! It grew right out of the ground. (The stage light brightens into daylight again.) Morning has finally arrived and now I can see the Easter Bunny and his friend just finished building a BEAUTIFUL EASTER EGG HILL!! It has a bright red door at the bottom.

THE EASTER BUNNY (calls out): Bobby, Sharon, come and see what we made for you!

(Bobby and Sharon come running out of the house.)

BOBBY: Oh my! An EASTER EGG HILL!! I never saw ANYTHING so BEAUTIFUL! YOU made THIS for US?

SHARON: Thank you! There is nothing ANYWHERE so BEAUTIFUL! (The children hug the two bunnies. They run up and down the hill. They look in through the open red door to see what is inside.)

BOBBY: There is a little room, just big enough for us. It has a table and chairs inside.

SUSY FLOWER: The Easter Bunny is giving each of them a gold key to the red door...but LOOK!   Here comes TROUBLE! Those MISCHIEVOUS BOYS again! and now THEY are running up and down the hill.

BOBBY: I'd better lock the red door to keep them from going inside!   (The mischievous boys scream!)

JAKE: I'm STUCK! My FEET are glued to the hill! All of a sudden, it HAPPENED!

BUD (cries and cries): I'm STUCK too! My feet are glued on so TIGHTLY! I can't pull them off! I'll be here forever! Let me GO! Let me GO! We'll be good!

EASTER BUNNY: I brought back the chocolate eggs to Bobby and Sharon, and you two boys can join our party IF you PROMISE to behave yourselves.

We can all be friends, but only if you behave.

BUD and JAKE (crying out): HELP US! HELP US! We're afraid! We don't want to stay stuck on this hill! We'll never be mean again! Please HELP us! Let us go!

EASTER BUNNY: Bobby and Sharon, shall we forgive them? Shall we give them another chance?

BOBBY: Yes! Let's all be friends!

SHARON: Easter time is for loving and forgiving. How can we get them off of our hill?

EASTER BUNNY: Open the locked red door and they will be free! No one can touch that door but YOU, Bobby and Sharon, because YOU carry the gold keys. If anyone else touches the Magic Door, he will stick there too, but when YOU open the door with the golden key, he will be free. As long as you carry those golden keys, you can never stick to the hill or door, and you both have the power to control the Easter Egg Hill. (Bobby opens the door and Bud and Jake run down the hill.)

BUD: Bobby, you are KING of EASTER EGG HILL and Sharon, you are the QUEEN. We can only play on the Easter Egg Hill when you open the door and INVITE us to play.

JAKE: We are sorry we were so mean. It is much more fun being friends.

EASTER BUNNY: Let's all have a party and share the chocolate eggs.

SHARON: Let's leave the door open and all have the party on top of our Easter Egg Hill! (Everyone CHEERS and they run to the top of Easter Egg Hill.)

CURTAIN

PRODUCTION NOTES:

The fence and house are cut out of painted cardboard. They are single-faced and attached just behind the front of the PUPPET STAGE. The hill prop is painted cardboard and the two bunnies building it are shown by dim rear lighting to appear as shadowy figures. The cart is a shadow silhouette that appears to be pulled on stage by the bunnies and then left off to the fence side, disappearing behind the curtains.

The bunnies run back and forth in the shadow, giving the appearance that they are getting eggs from the cart. The HILL PROP, as they build it, is pushed up slowly from below the stage, to appear to be growing. Then when it grows as high as you want it to be, clamp it INSIDE the FRONT of the stage. Leave space for the puppets. All puppets are operated from below. The puppets appear to run up and down the hill from behind it and appear over the edge. Children go into house (but really go behind it). Susy Flower puppet is operated through the open window, just below the windowsill. You can make Susy Flower as described in the SOCK PUPPET section of this book if you wish.

THE MAGIC WITCH
(USE HAND PUPPETS)

CHARACTERS:

GHOST, AS NARRATOR
WITCH
JIMMY
BILLY

TIME: The night before Halloween.
SETTING: The WITCH'S house and the STREET where she lives.

NOTE: This miniplay has all of the character's voices recorded on tape to be played back as the puppets perform.

THE PLAY

GHOST NARRATOR (stands center stage): It's a DARK and SCARY night. (He looks all around, as he talks.) Do YOU know WHERE we are? We are here on the street where the MAGIC WITCH lives, and THERE is her HOUSE! Halloween is ALMOST here. LOOK! Here she COMES. Here comes the MAGIC WITCH! The WITCH is coming out of her house. I hear the door creak. I'm going to hide. (THE GHOST DISAPPEARS. The WITCH comes out of her house. She mumbles.)
WITCH: Everywhere I go, the children ALL run away from me. It used to be fun, when I did mean magic TRICKS!

I used to scare people...but then.....I got so scared, I frightened myself. Those mean, magic tricks! They just aren't fun anymore! Now I want EVERYONE to LIKE me, to love me, LOVE ME, me, ME! What shall I DO? (The Witch cries and cries.) I haven't a friend in the WORLD!

GHOST (looking down from the roof): Oh, that poor brokenhearted Witch. She cries and walks back....and forth....and cries some more.

WITCH (to the audience): My face is so UGLY! Do you know what I need? I need a new face. THAT'S what I need! Do you know how I'll get a new face? Well I do! I'll make me a new face! I'll make a beautiful MASK to wear! THAT'S what I'll do. (The Witch goes into her house. Two boys appear, looking all around.)

JIMMY: Is THIS the street where the MAGIC WITCH lives? (They both shake with fear and cling to each other.)

BILLY: Yes, I think that she lives......RIGHT THERE!
JIMMY: Aren't you scared?

BILLY: Y-y-yes, but let's stay and see what happens. That's what Halloween is for.Isn't it?...and tomorrow IS Halloween!

JIMMY: .....to g-g-g-get scared! That's supposed to be the fun of it.

GHOST (peeks over fence): The Witch is coming out of her house at last. Why, she's wearing (HA, HA) a smiling, angelic mask! Oh my, oh MY! (The Ghost covers his mouth to suppress laughter. The two boys laugh and laugh.)

The WITCH cries out: OH DEAR ME! OH DEAR ME! (The Witch burst into tears and runs into her house.)

GHOST (shaking his head): There she goes....back inside her house, slamming the door. Poor thing!

BILLY: I wonder what she will do next? Will she do her mean magic tricks again? Will she try to scare us?

JIMMY: Get ready to run.....if she does....RUN FAST!

GHOST (sitting on the roof again, looks down):   Here comes the WITCH again! She's coming out of her house and wearing a FAIRY PRINCESS MASK! WHAT will she think of NEXT? She acts like she is very beautiful.

Hello, children, I have come to be your Halloween Princess. Aren't I beautiful? (The boys laugh and dance all about. The poor Witch cries and cries.)

WITCH: Oh dear me! What CAN I DO?

GHOST: The poor confused Witch hurries back into her house and shuts the door again. Very soon she reappears. This time the Witch comes out wearing a funny CLOWN MASK! She is hoping to make the children smile and be happy. The Witch speaks to the children.

WITCH: How about THIS mask? Do you like it?

The BOYS (screaming): She's MEAN again, she's MEAN again, just like she used to be. She's trying to scare us and be mean! That's what she's doing!

GHOST: The children run off quickly to hide behind the fence and the poor disappointed Witch walks sadly away and back into her house. She stays inside of the house a long, LONG time. The curious children finally come back on the street.

JIMMY: What happened to the Witch? Will she ever come out of her house again? I'm sorry we ran away. I think she was trying to be friends with us. A CLOWN mask isn't mean. Let's apologize to her.

BILLY: Let's knock on the door and see what happens. (He knocks on her door and waits.)

GHOST: Oh, oh, HERE SHE COMES out of her house carrying a large basket...and she is smiling! (The Ghost disappears.)

JIMMY (speaking to the Witch): You are not wearing a mask anymore?

WITCH: No, I've decided to bring all of you a nice surprise! I have made all of you and your friends HALLOWEEN MASKS!

GHOST (looking over the fence): The children in the neighborhood are very poor. They have no masks or costumes for Halloween. They will be so grateful to the Witch.(The boys and the Witch dance joyfully. The ghost dances on top of the fence.)

JIMMY: You have to spend Halloween with US!

BILLY: Please, WITCH, the children want to thank you for the masks and have you go TRICK or TREATING with us. Then we can have a party together and share what we get in our bags.

WITCH: Oh I am so happy! I'll never be lonely again.

JIMMY and BILLY: We want you to meet our families. (The boys leave with the Witch.) The Ghost claps his hands, comes out to the center stage, looks at the audience and says: Happy Halloween, everyone....Happy Halloween!

(He waves good-by.) Hey boys, wait for me! I want to meet your families, too. (The Ghost calls after the boys and the Witch and runs off the stage.)

CURTAIN

PRODUCTION NOTES:

The street, hills, sky, moon, stars, etc., are all painted on the backdrop. The Witch's house and fence are single-faced cardboard painted props that are attached just inside the front of the stage. The Witch goes BEHIND the house, but it appears that she is going into the house and later, out again.

THE LAND OF CHRISTMAS TOYS (A HAND PUP-PET PLAY)

(Record voices on TAPE to play as puppets perform.)

CHARACTERS: All are puppets except the live Holly.

HOLLY: (a live girl who acts OUTSIDE the theater)
HOLLY DOLL: (who looks like the live girl HOLLY)
CARROTTOP: (a rag doll)
SANTA CLAUS
NARRATOR: (who speaks behind the stage)
TOYS: (They are stick puppets.)
CANDY: (as STICK PUPPETS)
FAIRY TALE CHARACTERS: (They are STICK PUPPETS.)

TIME: Morning, the day before Christmas.

SETTING: SANTA'S TOY SHOP in a picture frame, hanging in Holly's living room. The live Holly is sitting on a chair near-by and Carrottop is on top of her chair with a puppeteer operating from behind, UNSEEN.

THE PLAY

NARRATOR: This is a story about wonderful things that happen at Christmas. Carrottop looks up at Santa's workshop, framed and hanging on the wall. Then Carrottop sighs and shakes Holly to wake her up.

CARROTTOP: Wake up Holly.

CARROTTOP (shakes Holly again): Wake up, Holly! I have a surprise for you! (Holly looks up amazed to see her doll talking to her.)

HOLLY: You moved! You talked! You're ALIVE! I always thought that MAYBE it could be true, but I didn't DARE to hope that it was!

CARROTTOP (pointing to the picture): We are ALL alive because you believe we are! All toys are alive! Look at your PICTURE on the wall. It's alive too! Santa and all of the toys in the picture are really alive! (The toys and Santa start moving.)

SANTA CLAUS (calls out): Holly, come and meet some of my toys. We finished early this year and thought you might like a few surprises before Christmas Eve. Very few children have been told that toys are really alive. We picked YOU this year because you believe we are.

SANTA (smiling): Meet the calico cat, the spotted dog, the checkered clown and the little green elf who helps me. His friends help me,too. (These toys walk in, one by one, and all the other toys say HELLO,too.)

SANTA (continues): What else would you like to see?

HOLLY: Your CANDY FACTORY!

SANTA CLAUS: We will take you there. The FRIENDLY CLOUD will help you. (A very large CLOUD peeks out from the back side of the puppet theater. Holly picks up the CLOUD by its stick handle and holds it in front of the stage like a curtain to block out the inside view as the scene is being changed. Then she puts back the CLOUD prop and she can look at the CANDY FACTORY interior scene.)

SANTA CLAUS: Here we are! (Candy cane stick puppets come marching in to say HELLO and giant stick puppet LOLLIPOPS...and a stick puppet jar of gumdrops with a face on the jar...)

HOLLY: (clapping with JOY!): Now can I go to the factory of FAIRY TALE BOOKS, too?

SANTA CLAUS: The FRIENDLY CLOUD will help you. (Holly picks up the CLOUD on a stick, as before, and holds it in front, covering the stage again as the scene is being changed to a CASTLE BOOK FACTORY BACKGROUND.)

HOLLY (smiling): A BOOK FACTORY in a CASTLE! How WONDERFUL! (The PRINCE and PRINCESS stick puppets appear to say HELLO......then a DWARF, and a WITCH, a BOY and GIRL, three PIGS, a friendly DRAGON....all say HELLO to Holly.)

HOLLY: All of my dreams have come true!

SANTA CLAUS: Now I have the BEST surprise of all for you. The FRIENDLY CLOUD will help you. (Holly gets the FRIENDLY CLOUD and holds it in front of the stage again as the scene is changed.)

SANTA CLAUS (calling out): We're READY! (Holly sets aside the CLOUD and looks into the picture frame.)

NARRATOR: The scene has turned into Santa's rooftop at the North Pole. His reindeer are waiting down below, but the sleigh is on the roof.

SANTA CLAUS: Holly, how would you like to become a HOLLY DOLL just for Christmas Eve? You and Carrottop can ride in my sleigh and ride all over the world this way. You have to be a toy to see how toys travel on Christmas Eve.

HOLLY: Oh YES, I'd love to be a DOLL and go!

SANTA CLAUS: Follow Carrottop and you can go. (A puppeteer moves Carrottop and Holly behind the puppet stage.)

NARRATOR: Then the HOLLY DOLL, dressed just like the real Holly, appears with Carrottop, sitting on Santa's SLEIGH. Santa calls his reindeer and they are harnessed and ready to go.

(Christmas music plays and the puppet stage darkens.)

SANTA and HOLLY (calling out): It's Christmas Eve and getting so dark. We'd better go.

HOLLY: (laughing): LOOK, LOOK! We're FLYING all over the world! I can see EVERYTHING as a DOLL!

SANTA CLAUS: We'll visit ALL of the boys and girls EVERYWHERE! Look Holly, there's YOUR HOUSE! (Christmas music plays again. The stage gradually lightens. The real live HOLLY is back, sitting on her chair next to the stage. She is holding and operating Carrottop.)

HOLLY: It's Christmas morning. What a wonderful Christmas Eve I had and Santa Claus showed me things no child has ever seen!...and real LIVE toys, just like you see in my picture. Those are the live TOYS!

HOLLY (smiles): Merry Christmas Carrottop! (Then to the audience she stands up and says): MERRY CHRISTMAS EVERYONE! (HOLLY and CARROTTOP wave and run off stage.)

CURTAIN

PRODUCTION NOTES:

The first scene is Santa's WORKSHOP (TOY SHOP). This is IN the PUPPET THEATER, which has a FRAME around it to make it look like a PAINTING hanging on the wall.

This scene is painted on the backdrop attached to a wire or rod and stays in place while the OTHER scenes are clipped on top of it and CHANGED.

THE SCENES

SANTA'S WORKSHOP

Make a cardboard CLOUD on a cardboard stick, large enough to cover the stage like a curtain when scenes are changed.

THE WORKSHOP backdrop has a window and door painted on it. The TABLE (with TOYS on it) is painted on a single-faced cardboard, attached inside the front of the stage. It must be easy to remove. TOYS are cardboard stick puppets.

SANTA'S CANDY FACTORY

Leave Santa's WORKSHOP scene in place; you will need it later. Hang the CANDY FACTORY backdrop on top of it.

229

It has a complete scene painted on it - a half open door to the factory, tall shelves of candy jars and a glass counter filled with trays of candies. A CANDY MAN stands behind the counter. All of this is painted on the backdrop. No PROP is needed.

A NEW FACTORY CASTLE

The CASTLE FACTORY is painted on the backdrop with hills and sky. A single-faced, cardboard painted stone wall is attached just inside the front of the stage.

SANTA'S ROOFTOP and SLEIGH

The scene of this backdrop has a gray-blue sky...just before darkness sets in and a moon and stars in yellow are painted on. Santa's reindeer are painted on a snowy hillside, just below the side of the roof.

THE ROOFTOP is a single-faced, cardboard painted prop with the red SLEIGH on top of it, and it is filled with colorful packages and toys. The HOUSE part that shows is a darker gray-blue, like a shadow effect, and has a yellow lighted window painted  on. The HOUSE and SLEIGH prop are attached just inside the front of the stage.

NOTE: The WORKSHOP backdrop stays in place as the other scenes are clipped on and removed each time, because the end of the play shows Santa's WORKSHOP AGAIN as when the play started. The FRAME around the stage opening can be cardboard, painted to look like a frame. Also, to save making so many puppets, use STICK PUPPETS as indicated in the play. They are just lightweight cardboard painted on, cut out and stapled to a cardboard stick or wire rod. CARROTTOP, SANTA, AND HOLLY ARE ALL HAND PUPPETS.

FIVE SONGS FOR PUPPETS TO PERFORM

TOTEM POLE
(with TOM-TOM accompaniment)

SIDE VIEW

Three children (as people puppets) make and wear colorful crepe paper Indian head masks. (See illustrations.) They act out this song described by its NUMBERS: (1) The three children run on stage to the musical beat of someone playing the TOM-TOM through the whole production. (2) Between (1) and (2) the children pile up, one above the other like a TOTEM POLE, but they MUST FACE THE AUDIENCE (see picture for positions). (3) After singing "THE TOTEM POLE" again, they climb OFF of each other and trot off the stage to the TOM-TOM beat. (4) Just before they disapppear, they sing "TOTEM POLE" with a WAR YELL.

"WHAT SHOULD I DO?"

A scene of children all talking together. Sue comes in and the children run away and hide, watching Sue. She sits on a couch and sings the FIRST PART of the song. Two puppeteers are hiding behind the couch, holding a MEAN RED PUPPET and a GOOD YELLOW PUPPET.

"WHAT SHOULD I DO?" (FIRST PART)

SUE SINGS, "WHAT SHOULD I DO? THEY DON'T LIKE ME— I WISH I KNEW HOW I SHOULD BE!"

MEAN RED PUPPET APPEARS and SPEAKS:

"Be like me, think me, me, ME!
Me first is what I say to be!
YES, push and pull and make them see
That I come first; think me, me, ME!!"

GOOD YELLOW PUPPET APPEARS and SPEAKS:

"No, no, oh no, that isn't so!
If you push and pull then your friends will go
So be good to them and they will know
This is how to start to make friendships grow.

234

SUE speaks: "YES, yes, yes!"

SUE SINGS THE SECOND PART:

(SECOND PART)

SUE SINGS: I KNOW WHAT TO DO, THEY WILL LIKE ME. I'LL BE GOOD TO THEM AND THEY'LL

BE GOOD TO ME."

Friends return to happily play with Sue. They dance and sing: "La, la, la,...." to the song's MELODY; then they all run off the stage.
The GOOD YELLOW PUPPET angrily HITS the MEAN RED PUPPET who FALLS backwards off the back of the couch and disappears behind it. The GOOD YELLOW PUPPET dusts off his hands with a gesture of "GOOD RIDDANCE!".... then waves good-by to the audience and also disappears behind the couch.

CURTAIN

MUSICAL NOTES SONG

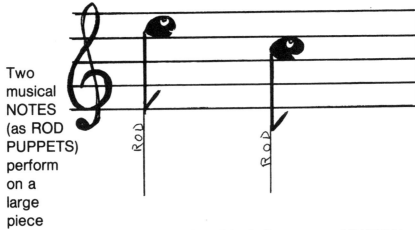

Two musical NOTES (as ROD PUPPETS) perform on a large piece of white cardboard. Rule five black lines as a MUSICAL STAFF for your NOTE PUPPETS to run up and down as they sing on the actual notes. (See the MUSIC.)

When they sing together, let them take turns on the staff. The two NOTES are black construction paper attached to RODS. At the end of the song, one NOTE chases the other NOTE down the scale, laughing as they run off of the musical page. (Puppets are operated from below.)

CURTAIN

NOTE: This can be educational for children. They learn notes and act out simple tunes.

THE MIRROR SONG

Choose two girls as "ME" PUPPETS. They will wear look-alike HEAD MASKS with crepe paper hair. Make holes to breathe and see and for their voices to come through. The STAGE is set with a dressing table and chair and an empty FRAME above it which appears as a MIRROR. One girl acts as the reflection. She hides behind the dressing table, waiting for her cue. The other girl plays the part of JEANNIE. Jeannie enters the stage, stamps her foot, and says: "I can't find my FRIENDSHIP RING. I left it on the dressing table. Now Carol won't speak to me, just because I can't find my friendship ring she gave me. Maybe it rolled onto the floor." Jeannie runs over to the dressing table and crawls around the floor looking for her ring. Then she stands up and sighs angrily: "I give UP. I can't find my friendship RING anywhere!"

Jeannie sits at the dressing table and as she sits, her reflection comes up, too, and imitates Jeannie. Then Jeannie SINGS and her reflection answers in the song.

THE MIRROR SONG

JEANNIE SINGS: IF YOU SMILE AT THE MIRROR IT SMILES AT YOU. IF YOU SCOWL AT THE MIRROR THEN IT WILL TOO. SO MOST PEOPLE LIKE MIRRORS YOU'LL FIND ITS

(HER REFLECTION SINGS)

TRUE, THEY WILL SMILE, OR THEY'LL SCOWL, THEY WILL ACT LIKE YOU.

Jeannie is surprised and says: "All right, now YOU can be my best friend." (They shake hands through the mirror. The reflection comes out, from behind the mirror frame. The girls hold hands and run off stage.)

CURTAIN

"POOR LITTLE ME!" (SONG)

(1) Little "ME" comes on stage and sings to her puppet. (2) The other children come on teasing and singing, then run off and hide, watching her from behind the fence. (3) "ME" is sorry to be so self-centered and sings the rest of the song.

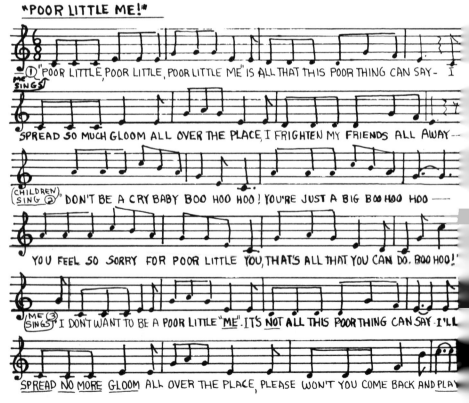

"POOR LITTLE ME!"

① "POOR LITTLE, POOR LITTLE, POOR LITTLE ME" IS ALL THAT THIS POOR THING CAN SAY- I
ME SINGS

SPREAD SO MUCH GLOOM ALL OVER THE PLACE, I FRIGHTEN MY FRIENDS ALL AWAY--

(CHILDREN SING ②) "DON'T BE A CRY BABY BOO HOO HOO! YOU'RE JUST A BIG BOO HOO HOO ----

YOU FEEL SO SORRY FOR POOR LITTLE YOU, THAT'S ALL THAT YOU CAN DO. BOO HOO!"

ME SINGS ③ I DON'T WANT TO BE A POOR LITTLE "ME". IT'S NOT ALL THIS POOR THING CAN SAY. I'LL

SPREAD NO MORE GLOOM ALL OVER THE PLACE, PLEASE WON'T YOU COME BACK AND PLAY

240

The children come back with their own puppets to play. (Their puppets were hidden behind the fence.) The children play "Follow the Leader" with puppets, following each other around and then off the stage.
Follow numbers (1), (2), (3) for acting out the SAME numbers in the song.

NOTE: Wonderful records and books to use: LOOK AT ME and LOOK AT THE HOLIDAYS
by Kathy Lecinski, Good Apple, Inc., Publishers.
Box 299, Carthage, Illinois   62321

PUPPETS CAN PLAY THE AUTOHARP

Hold your AUTOHARP so that the fingers of your right hand push down the CHORD BARS. Left hand for puppet strums across the strings with a large, strong hairpin that you insert through the INSIDE of the puppet's nose. The two ends of the HAIRPIN extend OUT of the NOSE and act as a PICK. This is easy to do, with the puppet strumming across the strings as you sing the songs and push down the chord bars to accompany yourself. Kathy Lecinski's two SONGBOOKS have all of the chords marked for each song. Use this idea for teaching or public performing with your HAND PUP-PETS.

SIX POEMS FOR PUPPETS TO PERFORM

MISS CROCODILE

NARRATOR off-stage, recites this poem as puppets act it out. The puppets' actions match the numbers in the poem.

SETTING

MISS CROCODILE (POEM)

(1) Miss CROCODILE cried to see who would come,
To catch him for her stew.....
BUT,
(2) When somebody came to Miss CROCODILE....
(3) He caught her for the ZOO!

PUPPET ACTIONS FOR THE POEM

(1) CROCODILE looks around smacking her lips.
She cries to attract attention to her.
(2) A HUNTER looks into the SCENE
from the side. The CROCODILE
smacks her lips,
and pretends
not
to
notice.

Then the HUNTER comes on stage partway. CROCODILE hurries to gobble him up.

(3) HUNTER throws his net over her, which was not seen until the last moment by the audience. The HUNTER and CROCODILE inside net go off together.

CURTAIN

PRODUCTION NOTES:

You can use a long green SOCK with green felt glued on top to make MISS CROCODILE. Your hand goes inside her mouth to move it. Glue on felt legs. The HUNTER is a regular hand puppet. He holds a huge NET, sewed to his hand.
SCENERY: The water-effect prop is painted on cardboard attached just inside the front of stage. The JUNGLE scene is painted on the BACKDROP.

LET'S PLAY

NARRATOR off-stage recites this poem as two CHILDREN HAND PUPPETS act it out. The puppets' actions match the numbered lines of the poem.

PLAYROOM SETTING –

LET'S PLAY (POEM)

(1) Two children played in a playroom one day.
(2) Each was determined to have his own way.
(3) So they played in two corners, sad and alone.
(4) Then said, "It's no fun, let's share what we own."

PUPPET ACTIONS FOR THE POEM

(1) Two puppet children playing and moving about.
(2) Suddenly the children push and shove and fight.
(3) They each play in opposite corners, ALONE.
(4) Then, the puppets come together to share toys.

CURTAIN

Each child hand puppet has a toy temporarily stitched to one hand for this poem.
THE SCENE: It is completely painted on the backdrop (window, toy chest and toys).

A BUNNY IN A HOLE

NARRATOR, off-
stage, recites
this poem as a
paper BUTTERFLY
on a rod acts

SETTING

it out. The puppets' actions match the numbered lines of this poem.

A BUNNY IN A HOLE (POEM)

(1) A BUNNY fell down a very deep hole,
(2) With no one to help him, nary a soul.
(3) At first he said "Can't," and couldn't that's why.
(4) But finally climbed out, when he started to try.

"I CAN, I CAN, I CAN, I CAN, I CAN!"

PUPPET ACTIONS FOR THE POEM

(1) Bunny hops happily after a BUTTERFLY and falls into a hole.
(2) He tries to climb out, but he slips and slides to the bottom again.
(3) Bunny shakes his head to say "No."
(4) He hops again, runs up one side, slides down and gains enough momentum to run right up the other side and out. He happily runs away.

CURTAIN

PRODUCTION NOTES: (for BUNNY IN A HOLE....POEM)

Observe picture. Cut the ground and deep-hole effect out of cardboard. Paint the grass on top bright green. The ground area around hole is a dark brown silhouette effect. Fasten it just behind the front inside of stage. Paint the backdrop light blue sky color for a contrast.

MAKE HAND PUPPET BUNNY of white fake fur or a white velour hand towel. The BUTTERFLY is stiff paper, colored, with a chenille stem folded around the middle of body and then folded under to fasten to rod. Lean butterfly toward Bunny from other side. He flies off as Bunny falls in hole. Bunny moves easily from behind ground prop, sliding up and down, then out. He appears to be on the ground.

ROD

THE BEAR AND
THE LADYBUG

NARRATOR off-
stage, recites
this poem as
the bear and
hunter act out
their parts.

The puppets' actions match the numbered lines of the poem.

THE BEAR AND THE LADYBUG (POEM)

(1) Oh, that big fuzzy bear, he made quite a to-do
(2) When a BUG on his nose caused a great big "kerchoo."
(3) She begged for her life. Then the bear said, "O.K." "Oh thank you, big bear, such a debt I'll repay!"

Then,

(4) A HUNTER appeared. What did the bug do?
(5) She tickled his nose and made HIM "KERCHOO!"
(6) This WARNED the big bear; he ran quickly away!
(7) The BEAR thanked the BUG; they are friends to this day.

PUPPET ACTIONS FOR THIS POEM

(1) Bear hears a buzzing sound and looks around.
(2) He tries to shoo the BUG away with his paw. Bear sneezes.
(3) Bug's voice says: "Please don't hurt me!" Bear cocks his ear to listen.

(4) HUNTER peeks out from the side.

(5) HUNTER sneezes! This makes the Bear turn to see the HUNTER.

(6) The Bear runs to hide.

(7) Bear comes back. Hunter is gone.

CURTAIN

PRODUCTION NOTES:

Make the BEAR hand puppet of fake brown fur. Your hand goes inside mouth to move it, and your other hand moves Bear's paw by holding a rod sewed to the paw to shoo away the bug. The tiny bug is not seen by the audience. The bug's high voice can be heard and the Bear's actions give the illusion that the bug is there. The Bear swats at the unseen bug with his paw and snaps at her with his mouth. HUNTER is also a hand puppet. The FOREST SCENE is painted on the backdrop.

THE JEALOUS
LITTLE FLOWER

NARRATOR, off-
stage, recites
this poem as
the flowers
act out their
parts. The puppets' actions match the numbered lines of the
poem.

THE JEALOUS LITTLE FLOWER (POEM)

(1) The jealous little flower said, "Down you go! No flower
more beautiful than I should grow!"
(2) So they all disappeared, she grew lonesome and sad.

BUT

(3) In SPRING (4) They came back, and then she was glad!

PUPPET ACTIONS FOR THIS POEM

(1) Flower scolds and shakes head angrily at the other
flowers.
(2) Flowers disappear downward and then the jealous little
flower disappears too.
(3) On word SPRING, the jealous little flower comes up
again and looks around.

251

(4) On words "THEY CAME BACK," the other flowers come up too, and they are all happy.

CURTAIN

PRODUCTION NOTES:

The jealous little flower has a scowl on her face, but later when she comes back in the spring, her smiling face painted on the other side shows. The other flowers grow up again. A puppeteer holds two flowers in each hand by their long green wire stems. Both puppeteers work from below the stage. All flowers are made like STICK PUPPETS on green rods (their stems).
THE GARDEN SCENERY is painted on the backdrop.

THE HAPPY PLUM TREE

NARRATOR, off-
stage, recites
this poem
as the puppets
act out their
parts. The
puppets' actions match the numbered lines of the poem.

THE HAPPY PLUM TREE (POEM)

Said one little plum in a happy plum tree,
(1) "I'm better than you, for I only need ME!"
(2) He hopped to the ground and dried up quite SOON,
(3) And there he became a lonely OLD PRUNE.

PUPPET ACTIONS FOR THIS POEM

(1) Plum moves up and down.
(2) Plum hops out of tree onto the ground.
(3) Plum moves a little on the ground.
(4) Boy picks up PLUM and walks off with the plum.

CURTAIN

PRODUCTION NOTES:

A tree cut out of cardboard is fastened just inside the front of
the stage.

Its leaves are painted green and it has many purple plums with faces painted with happy smiles. The little plum who brags is separate and has a proud but grouchy face. He may be cut out of cardboard or made out of a Ping-Pong ball painted purple. Be sure the WHITES of all the plums' eyes show. Attach a rod to the grouchy plum that the puppeteer holds from below, to move him to the ground. At the end of the poem, a little hand puppet BOY comes along, picks up the plum and walks off with him. The BACKDROP is blue sky, hills, etc., painted on.